The Absolute Beginner's Guide to Python Programming

A Step-by-Step Guide with Examples and Lab Exercises

Kevin Wilson

Apress®

The Absolute Beginner's Guide to Python Programming: A Step-by-Step Guide with Examples and Lab Exercises

Kevin Wilson
London, UK

ISBN-13 (pbk): 978-1-4842-8715-6   ISBN-13 (electronic): 978-1-4842-8716-3
https://doi.org/10.1007/978-1-4842-8716-3

Copyright © 2022 by Kevin Wilson

Managing Director, Apress Media LLC: Welmoed Spahr
Acquisitions Editor: Celestin Suresh John
Development Editor: James Markham
Coordinating Editor: Shrikant Vishwakarma

Cover designed by eStudioCalamar

Cover image by Shutterstock

Distributed to the book trade worldwide by Apress Media, LLC, 1 New York Plaza, New York, NY 10004, U.S.A. Phone 1-800-SPRINGER, fax (201) 348-4505, e-mail orders-ny@springer-sbm.com, or visit www.springeronline.com. Apress Media, LLC is a California LLC and the sole member (owner) is Springer Science + Business Media Finance Inc (SSBM Finance Inc). SSBM Finance Inc is a **Delaware** corporation.

For information on translations, please e-mail booktranslations@springernature.com; for reprint, paperback, or audio rights, please e-mail bookpermissions@springernature.com.

Apress titles may be purchased in bulk for academic, corporate, or promotional use. eBook versions and licenses are also available for most titles. For more information, reference our Print and eBook Bulk Sales web page at http://www.apress.com/bulk-sales.

Any source code or other supplementary material referenced by the author in this book is available to readers on GitHub (https://github.com/Apress). For more detailed information, please visit http://www.apress.com/source-code.

Printed on acid-free paper

Table of Contents

About the Author xi

About the Technical Reviewer xiii

Introduction xv

Chapter 1: Introduction to Computer Programming 1

What Is Python 2

Getting Started 4

Setting Up 4

Install on Windows 4

Install on MacOS 9

Install on Linux 11

Summary 13

Chapter 2: The Basics 15

Language Classification 15

Low-Level Language 15

High-Level Language 16

Python Language Syntax 18

Reserved Words 18

Identifiers 20

Indentation 20

Comments 20

Input 21

Output..21

Escape Characters..21

Writing a Program..22

Lab Exercises...29

Summary..30

Chapter 3: Working with Data 31

Variables..31

Local Variables..31

Global Variables..32

Basic Data Types..32

Integers..32

Floating Point Numbers...33

Strings..33

Lists..33

Two-Dimensional Lists...35

Sets..37

Tuples...37

Dictionaries..38

Program Input...39

Program Output..40

Casting Data Types..41

Arithmetic Operators..42

Operator Precedence..42

Performing Arithmetic...43

Comparison Operators..43

Boolean Operators..44

Bitwise Operators 45

Lab Exercises 45

Summary...46

Chapter 4: Flow Control 49

Sequence 49

Selection 52

if... else 52

elif..55

Iteration (Loops) 61

For Loop..61

While Loop 65

Break and Continue..68

Lab Exercises 69

Summary...69

Chapter 5: Handling Files 71

File Types 71

Text File 71

Binary 72

Text File Operations..73

Open Files..73

Write to a File 75

Read from a File 78

Binary File Operations...79

Open Files..79

Write to a File 80

Read a File...81

Random File Access 83

Lab Exercises 84

Summary 85

Chapter 6: Using Functions 87

Declaring Functions 87

Scope 90

Recursion 90

    Lab Exercises 92

Summary 93

Chapter 7: Using Modules 95

Importing Modules 96

Creating Your Own Modules 100

Lab Exercises 101

Summary 102

Chapter 8: Exception Handling 103

Types of Exception 103

Catching Exceptions 105

Raising Your Own Exceptions 107

Summary 108

Chapter 9: Object-Oriented Programming 109

Principles of OOP 109

    Encapsulation 109

    Inheritance 110

    Polymorphism 110

    Abstraction 110

Classes and Objects..110

Class Inheritance 113

Polymorphic Classes..116

Method Overriding 117

Lab Exercises...119

Summary...120

Chapter 10: Building an Interface...121

Creating a Window 121

Adding Widgets 124

    Menus...124

    The Canvas 126

    Images..129

    Buttons..130

    Message Boxes 131

    Text Field 132

    Listbox..133

    Checkbox..135

    Labels...137

    Label Frame..138

Interface Design...139

Summary...144

Chapter 11: Developing a Game..145

Installing Pygame...145

Opening a Window 147

Adding an Image 148

The Game Loop 149

The Event Loop 151

Shapes 155

Basic Animation 156

Summary... 164

Chapter 12: Python Web Development 167

Web Servers.. 167

Install the Web Server... 169

Set Up Python Support... 169

Executing a Script... 171

Python Web Frameworks 175

Summary... 181

Appendix A: Quick Reference 183

Data Types... 183

Numeric Operators... 183

Comparison Operators 184

Boolean Operators 184

String Operators... 184

List Operators... 184

Dictionary Operators 185

String Methods... 185

List Methods 185

Dictionary Methods.. 185

Functions 186

Files 186

Conditional 186

Multi-conditional.. 186

While Loop 187

For Loop 187

Loop Control 187

Modules 187

Built-In Functions..187

Declare a Class 188

Child Class 188

Create Object 188

Call Object Method...188

Access Object Attributes 188

Exceptions...188

Index..189

About the Author

With over 20 years' experience in the computer industry, **Kevin Wilson** has made a career out of technology and showing others how to use it. After earning a master's degree in computer science, software engineering, and multimedia systems, Kevin has held various positions in the IT industry including graphic and web design, digital film and photography, programming and software engineering, developing and managing corporate networks, building computer systems, and IT support. He currently teaches computer science at college and works as an IT trainer in England while researching for his Ph.D.

About the Technical Reviewer

 **Joos Korstanje** is a data scientist, with over five years of industry experience in developing machine-learning tools. He has a double M.Sc. in applied data science and environmental science and has extensive experience working with geodata use cases. He currently works at Disneyland Paris, where he develops machine learning for a variety of tools. His project experience includes forecasting, recommender engines, optimization, machine learning on GPS tracking data, and more. Joos is also an active blogger on Medium and has worked on multiple book publications.

Introduction

The aim of this book is to provide a first course in the use of Python to develop programs.

It provides a foundation for those who wish to write computer programs based on sound programming principles, and because the book is intended to be a primer, it allows the beginner to become comfortable with basic programming tasks.

As it is a first course, no previous experience of computer programming is assumed.

Throughout the book, we'll explore the Python programming language with worked examples and lab exercises for you to complete yourself. For this purpose, we've included all the source code for this book in the following repository: github.com/apress/absolute-beginners-guide-python

## CHAPTER 1

Introduction to Computer Programming

What is a computer program? A computer is a device that processes instructions to achieve a task. This set of instructions is called a computer program.

A computer program usually takes some data such as a string or a number and performs calculations to produce results. We usually refer to the data as the program's input and the results as the program's output.

To write computer programs, we use a computer programming language. There are many different languages such as BASIC, C, C++, and Python. In this guide, we are going to concentrate on the Python programming language.

Every computer program manipulates data to produce a result, so most languages allow the programmer to choose names for each item of data. These items are called variables or constants. A variable, as the name suggests, is an item that can contain different values as the program is executed. A constant stays the same.

© Kevin Wilson 2022
K. Wilson, *The Absolute Beginner's Guide to Python Programming*,
https://doi.org/10.1007/978-1-4842-8716-3_1

For example, if we wrote a program to calculate the volume of a sphere, we could have variables for the radius and one for the result. We can also have a constant for the value of Pi as it never changes.

In larger programs, we often need to make decisions based on user input, a calculated result, or condition. In this case, we use an if statement. This is called selection.

Some blocks of code might also need to be repeated; in this case, we use a loop. This is called repetition.

The Python programming language has specific facilities to enable us to implement the concepts outlined earlier. Many of these will be introduced throughout this book.

What Is Python

Python is a high-level language developed by Guido van Rossum in the late 1980s and is used in web development, scientific applications, gaming, AI, and is well suited to education for teaching computer programming.

Python is designed to be an easily readable language. Therefore, it uses an uncluttered formatting style and often uses English keywords where other languages use a symbol.

Python is an interpreted programming language, meaning Python programs are written in a text editor and then put through a Python interpreter to be executed.

Python is used in the field of artificial intelligence and can be found in many day-to-day applications. Streaming services such as Spotify use Python for data analysis, particularly users' listening habits in order to offer suggestions on which artist to follow, other music a particular user might be interested in, and so on. Python is also used within Netflix's machine-learning algorithms for recommending relevant content to users, monitoring browsing habits, and marketing.

In the world of games development, Python is used as a companion language, meaning Python scripts are used to add customizations to the core gaming engine, script AI behaviors, or server side elements. The performance of Python isn't fast enough for coding graphics-intensive, higher-end games; however, you can create simple games with Python using the pygame module.

Python is used in web development and allows a web developer to develop dynamic web apps very quickly.

Python is a multi-platform language and is available for Windows, MacOS, Linux, and the Raspberry Pi.

To start coding, you'll need a computer – either Windows, MacOS, or Linux – and an integrated development environment (IDE) with the Python interpreter.

Getting Started

In this section, we'll take a look at how to install the Python interpreter and development environment. You can install Python on Windows, Mac, or Linux.

Setting Up

Before we start writing programs, we need to set up our development environment. We'll take a look at installing Python on Windows, Mac, and Linux.

Install on Windows

In our lab, we're using Windows workstations, so we'll need to install the Python integrated development environment for Windows.

Open your web browser and navigate to the following website:

`www.python.org/downloads/windows`

From the Downloads page, select the "executable installer" of the latest stable release.

Python Releases for Windows

- Latest Python 3 Release - Python 3.7.3
- Latest Python 2 Release - Python 2.7.16

Stable Releases

- Python 3.7.3 - March 25, 2019
  Note that Python 3.7.3 *cannot* be used on Windows XP or earlier.

  - Download Windows help file
  - Download Windows x86-64 embeddable zip file
  - Download Windows x86-64 executable installer
  - Download Windows x86-64 web-based installer
  - Download Windows x86 embeddable zip file
  - Download Windows x86 executable installer
  - Download Windows x86 web-based installer
- Python 3.4.10 - March 18, 2019
  - No files for this release.
- Python 3.5.7 - March 18, 2019
  Note that Python 3.5.7 *cannot* be used on Windows XP or earlier.

  - No files for this release.
- Python 2.7.16 - March 4, 2019
  - Download Windows debug information files
  - Download Windows debug information files for 64-bit binaries
  - Download Windows help file
  - Download Windows x86-64 MSI installer

Pre-releases

- Python 3.8.0a4 - May 6, 2019
  - Download Windows help file
  - Download Windows x86-64 embeddable zip file
  - Download Windows x86-64 executable installer
  - Download Windows x86-64 web-based installer
  - Download Windows x86 embeddable zip file
  - Download Windows x86 executable installer
  - Download Windows x86 web-based installer
- Python 3.8.0a3 - March 25, 2019
  - Download Windows help file
  - Download Windows x86-64 embeddable zip file
  - Download Windows x86-64 executable installer
  - Download Windows x86-64 web-based installer
  - Download Windows x86 embeddable zip file
  - Download Windows x86 executable installer
  - Download Windows x86 web-based installer
- Python 3.7.3rc1 - March 12, 2019
  - Download Windows help file
  - Download Windows x86-64 embeddable zip file
  - Download Windows x86-64 executable installer

Click "run" when prompted by your browser. Or click "python-x.x.x-amd64.exe" if you're using Chrome.

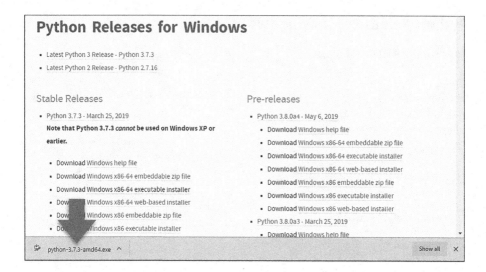

Once the installer starts, make sure "Add Python 3.x to PATH" is selected, and then click "Customize installation" to run through the steps to complete the installation.

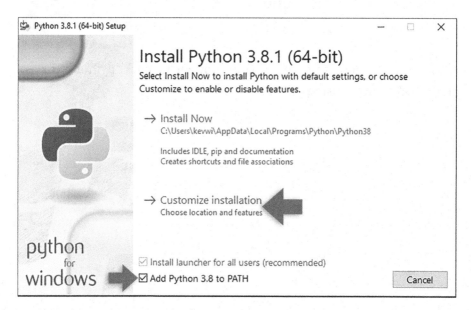

Make sure you select all the tick boxes for all the optional features.

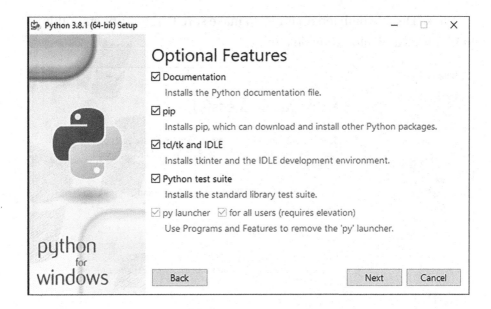

Click "Next."

Make sure "Install for all users" is selected at the top of the dialog box. Click "Install" to begin.

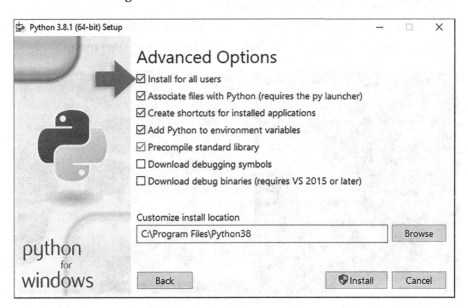

Click "Disable path length limit" to make sure Python runs smoothly on Windows and allow long filenames.

Click "Close" to finish the installation.

You'll find the Python integrated development environment (IDLE) and the Python interpreter in the Python folder on your start menu.

To write our programs, we'll use IDLE Python. This is Python's integrated development environment.

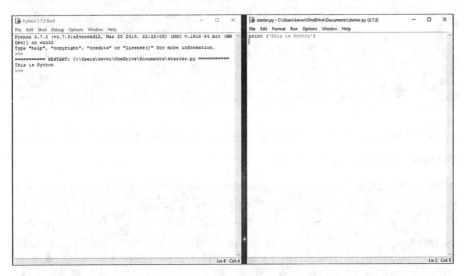

Here, you can write your code in the editor and then execute and debug your code. You'll also notice the code editor provides syntax highlighting, meaning keywords and text are highlighted in different colors, making code easier to read.

Install on MacOS

To install Python 3 with the official installer, open your web browser and navigate to the following website:

`www.python.org/downloads/macos`

Click Download Python.

You'll find the package in your Downloads folder. Double-click on the package to begin the installation.

Run through the installation wizard. Click "Continue."

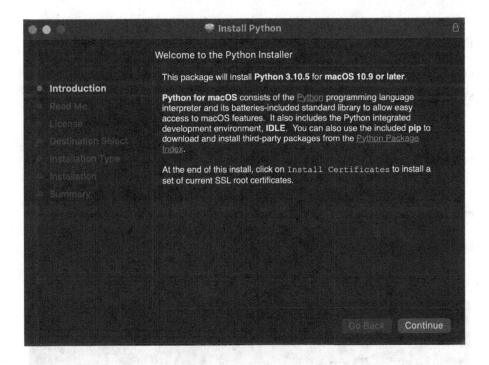

Once the installation is complete, you'll find Python in the Applications folder in Finder or on the launchpad.

Install on Linux

If you are running a Linux distribution such as Ubuntu or have a Raspberry Pi, you can install Python using the terminal. You'll find the terminal app in your applications. You can also press **Control+Alt+T** on your keyboard.

At the terminal command prompt, type the following commands. Press Enter after each line.

```
sudo apt update
sudo apt upgrade
```

Type the following command to install Python:

```
sudo apt install python3 -y
```

Once the Python is installed, we need to install IDLE, the development environment. To do this, type the following command at the prompt:

```
sudo apt-get install idle3 -y
```

Once installed, you'll find IDLE in your applications.

Or you can type the following command at the prompt:

```
idle
```

Arrange your windows so you can see your code window and the shell.

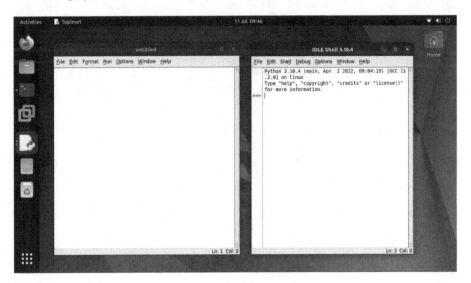

Summary

- Python is a high-level language whose code is executed by an interpreter to produce output.

- Python is a multi-platform language and is available for Windows, MacOS, Linux, and the Raspberry Pi.

- To write our programs, we use IDLE Python. This is Python's integrated development environment.

CHAPTER 2

The Basics

Python programs are written in a text editor, such as Notepad, PyCharm, or the code editor in Python's integrated development environment (IDLE), and saved with a .py file extension.

You then use the Python interpreter to execute the code saved in the file.

Let's start at the beginning.

Language Classification

There are different levels of programming language: low-level languages and high-level languages.

Low-Level Language

A low-level language is a programming language whose functions often refer directly to the processor's instructions and is commonly written in machine code or assembly language. Assembly language is known as a second-generation programming language, machine code being the first generation.

Let's take a look at a simple program. Here, we have a little adder program written in assembly language for our processor, and might look something like this:

© Kevin Wilson 2022
K. Wilson, *The Absolute Beginner's Guide to Python Programming*,
https://doi.org/10.1007/978-1-4842-8716-3_2

LDA 12H

ADD 07H

STA 09H

STP

Code is written in assembly language and then assembled into machine code using an assembler before it is executed.

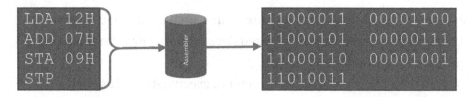

Figure 2-1. *Code assembled into machine code by assembler*

Each assembly language instruction corresponds to a sequence of binary numbers in machine code. The numbers, characters, addresses, and other data are converted into their machine code equivalents.

So, LDA could be represented by the binary code 11000011; the number 12_{10} is 00001100 in binary.

The assembled machine code is then executed by the processor.

High-Level Language

Python is an example of a high-level language. Rather than dealing directly with processor registers and memory addresses, high-level languages deal with variables, human-readable statements, loops, and functions.

High-level language code is either compiled into a machine code executable program or interpreted. Languages such as C or C++ are often compiled, meaning the code is written and then converted into an executable file. This makes them ideal for software development to write applications such as Microsoft Word that run on a computer.

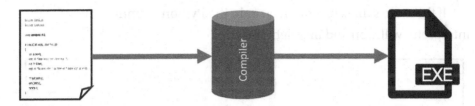

Figure 2-2. *Code compiled into machine code by compiler*

Python is an interpreted language, meaning the code you write is translated into machine code directly, making it well suited to web development.

Here, you can see the interpreter executes the code line by line while accessing any data required by the program and then displays the output directly onto the screen.

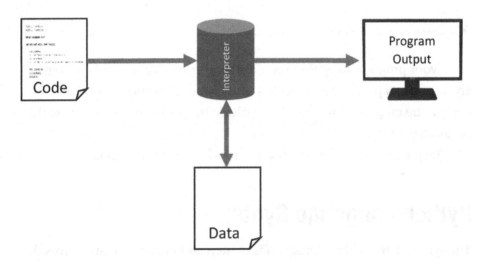

Figure 2-3. *Code interpreted by interpreter for execution*

When you attempt to run your program, the interpreter will convert and execute your code, but will only do this if it doesn't contain any errors.

If there are syntax errors, an error in the Python grammar, the interpreter will stop and highlight the error.

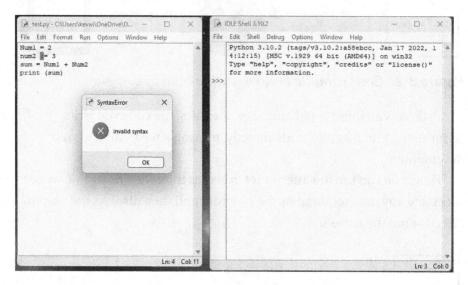

If your program runs, there could still be errors. These could be logical errors and can produce unexpected results and are sometimes called bugs in the program. This could be a divide by 0 error which can cause the program to crash.

The process of eliminating these errors is called debugging.

Python Language Syntax

The syntax defines how a program is written and interpreted and forms the basis of writing code.

Reserved Words

These are words reserved by the programming language that define the syntax and structure. Here are some of the most common ones:

and	A logical operator commonly used in if statements
as	Creates an alias
assert	For testing conditions and used in debugging
break	Breaks out of a loop
class	Creates a class
continue	Continues to the next iteration of a loop
def	Defines a function
del	Deletes an object
elif	Used in conditional statements, same as else if
else	Used in conditional statements
except	Defines code to run when error occurs (an exception)
false	Boolean value, result of comparison operations
finally	Used with exceptions, a block of code that will be executed no matter if there is an exception or not
for	Creates a for loop
from	Used to import only a specified section from a module.
global	Declares a global variable
if	Create a conditional statement
import	Imports a module
in	Used to check if a value is present in a sequence
is	Used to test if two variables refer to the same object
lambda	Used to create small anonymous functions
None	Represents a null value
nonlocal	Used to work with variables inside nested functions,
not	A logical operator
or	A logical operator
pass	Does nothing, used as a placeholder
raise	Used to raise an exception.
return	To exit a function and return a value
true	Boolean value, result of comparison operations
try	To make a try...except statement
while	Creates a while loop
with	Used to simplify exception handling
yield	Used to end a function, returns a generator

For example, the word "while" indicates a while loop. The word "if" defines an "if statement." You can't use a reserved word as a variable name or function name.

Identifiers

An identifier is a name given to a class, function, or a variable. Identifiers can be a combination of uppercase or lowercase letters, numbers, or an underscore (_). Try to keep the identifiers meaningful, so that they describe what they're used for.

printData, firstVariable, _count, userCount

Indentation

Most other programming languages such as C and C++ use braces { } to define a block of code. Python uses indentation. Use the tab key.

C++	Python

if test condition {
    execute this block if true;
} else {
    otherwise execute this block;
{
	if test condition:
	    execute this block if true
	else:
	    otherwise execute this block

Comments

A comment is an explanation or annotation in the source code of a computer program for the purpose of making the source code easier for other programmers to understand. Comments are intended to be human readable for the programmer's benefit and are ignored by the Python interpreter during execution.

Comments are very important while writing a program. You should clearly document all your code using comments, so other developers working on a project can better understand what your code is doing.

Use the hash character (#) to write single-line comments:

```
# Prompt user for two numbers
a = input ('Enter first number: ')
b = input ('Enter second number: ')
```

If you need to write a block describing the functionality, then use a triple quote before and after the comment block.

For example:

```
""" Prompt user for two numbers
one after the other using a text input """
a = input ('Enter first number: ')
b = input ('Enter second number: ')
```

Input

You can obtain input from the user using the input( ) function. This function prompts the user to type in some data.

```
number = input ('Enter a number: ')
```

Output

You can display information on the screen with the print( ) function. You can print the contents of a variable or enclose a string within the parameters of the print( ) function. For example:

```
print (number)
```

Escape Characters

An escape character tells the interpreter to perform a specific operation such as a line break or tab or a reserved character such as a quote mark or apostrophe.

Escape characters start with the a backslash (\) and are used to format a string. Table 2-1 lists escape characters and their function.

Table 2-1. *Escape characters*

Escape Character	Function
\n	Line break
\t	Tab (horizontal indentation)
\	New line in a multiline string
\\	Backslash
\'	Apostrophe or single quote
\"	Double quote ·

For example, you could use the tab escape and break line character to format some text:

print("John \t 45 \nJoanne \t 15")

The output to this line would look something like this:

John   45
Joanne   15

Writing a Program

To write a program, open IDLE Python from the start menu. Select the File menu and then click "New File."

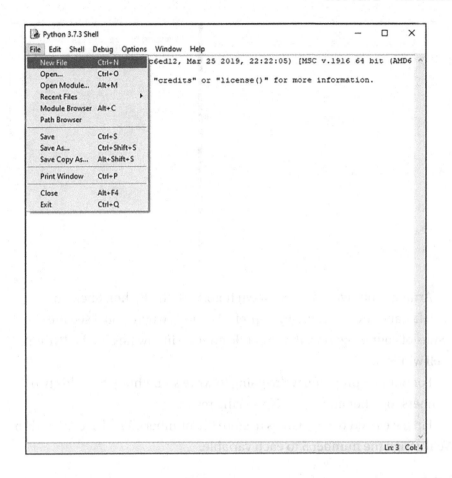

A new blank window will appear. This is the code editor. Here, you can write all your Python code.

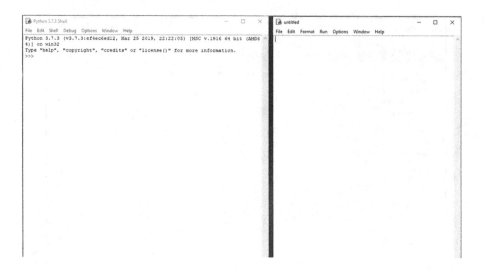

Arrange your windows as shown here, with the Python Shell on the left-hand side (or right if you prefer) – this is where you'll see the results of your programs. Put the code editor window next to the Python Shell window.

For our first program, we're going to write something that adds two numbers together and then displays the result.

First, we need two variables to store the numbers. We'll use "a" and "b." We'll assign the number 5 to each variable.

```
a = 5
b = 5
```

Next, we need a piece of code that will add the two numbers together and store the result. In this case, the values assigned to the variables "a" and "b" will be added together and stored in the variable "result."

```
result = a + b
```

Next, we'll need a function to print the result on the screen:

```
print (result)
```

Let's put it all together in a program.

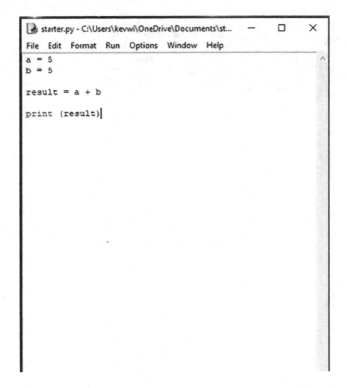

To run the program, press F5, or go to the "Run" menu in your code editor and click "Run Module."

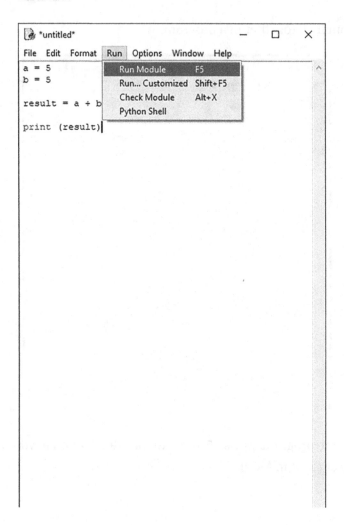

You can see in the following image the output of the program, in this case "10."

This particular program isn't very useful. It would be much better if we could allow the user to enter the numbers they want to add together. To do this, we'll need to add a function that will prompt the user for a value.

We'll use the **input** function. We can replace the variables "a" and "b" from the previous program with the input function.

```
a = input ('Enter first number: ')
b = input ('Enter second number: ')
```

Now, because the input function reads the values entered as text (called a string), we need to convert these to numbers. So we need to modify the code that adds the two numbers together. We can use the **int** function – this converts the text to an integer which is a fancy name for a whole number.

```
result = int(a) + int(b)
```

Let's put it all together in a program.

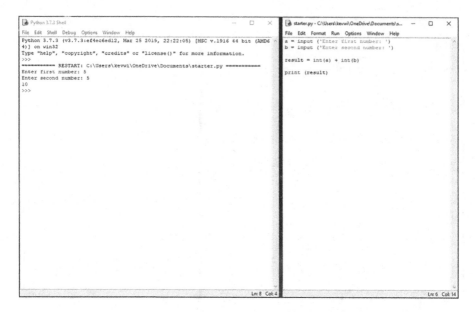

You can see in the following image the output of the program. The program prompted the user for two numbers, added them together, and then displayed the result underneath.

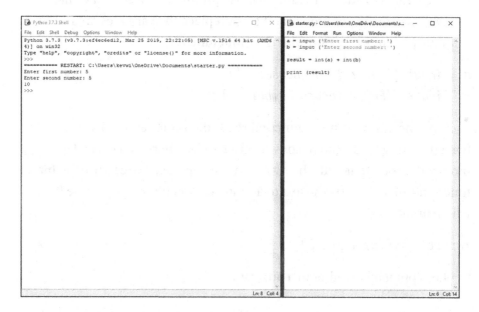

Lab Exercises

What is the output produced by the following code fragment?

```
num1 = 2
num2 = 3
print (num1 + num2)
```

What is the output produced by the following code fragment?

```
num1 = 2
num2 = 3
print ("num 1 + num 2 = ", num1 + num2)
```

Find the errors in the following program:

```
Num1 = 2
num2 := 3
Sum = num1 + num2;
printf(sum)
```

Which of the following identifiers are valid and which are invalid? Why?

```
Num1
time-of-day
tax_rate
x5
int
7th_Rec
yield
```

How do you write comments in your code? Explain with an example. Why should you include comments?

Summary

- Python programs are written in a text editor, such as Notepad, PyCharm, or the code editor in Python's development environment (IDLE), and saved with a .py file extension.

- Python is an example of a high-level language.

- Python is an interpreted language, meaning the code you write is translated into machine code directly, making it well suited to web development.

- An identifier is a name given to a class, function, or a variable.

- Python uses indentation to mark a block of code. Use the tab key to indent.

- A comment is an explanation or annotation in the source code of a computer program for the purpose of making the source code easier for other programmers to understand.

- You can obtain input from the user using the input( ) function.

- You can display information on the screen with the print( ) function.

CHAPTER 3

Working with Data

You can store and manipulate all different types of data: a number, a string, list, and so on. With Python, you don't need to declare all your variables before you use them.

Variables

A variable is a labeled location in memory that is used to store values within a computer program. There are two types of variables: local and global.

Local Variables

Variables defined within a function are called local variables, as they are local to that particular function. These variables can only be seen by the function in which they are defined. These variables have local scope. Figure 3-1 shows an example of local variables.

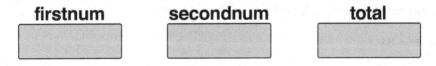

Figure 3-1. *An example of local variables*

K. Wilson, *The Absolute Beginner's Guide to Python Programming*,
https://doi.org/10.1007/978-1-4842-8716-3_3

Global Variables

Global variables are defined in the main body of the program outside any particular functions. These variables can be seen by any function and are said to have global scope.

Here in the example below, "a" and "b" are global variables, while "firstnum," "secondnum," and "sum" are local variables.

```
a = int(2)
b = int(3)
def addsum(firstnum, secondnum):
    sum = firstnum + secondnum
    return sum
```

You would not be able to access the variables "firstnum," "secondnum," and "sum" from outside the "addnum" function.

Basic Data Types

A variable can store various types of data, called a data type. Let's introduce some of the basic types we'll be looking at.

Integers

An integer is a whole number and can be positive or negative. Integers can usually be of unlimited length.

```
score = 45
```

Floating Point Numbers

A floating point number, sometimes called a real number, is a number that has a decimal point:

```
temperature = 44.7
```

Strings

In Python code, a string must be enclosed in quotes "..." or '...':

```
name = "John Myers"
```

Lists

A list is an ordered sequence of data items usually of the same type, each identified by an index (shown in the circles). This is known as a one-dimensional list.

Lists are known as arrays in other programming languages, and you can create one like this – list elements are enclosed in square brackets [ ]:

```
shoppingList = ['bread', 'milk', 'coffee', 'cereal']
```

To reference an item in a list, put the reference in square brackets:

```
print (shoppingList[1])
```

You can assign another value to an item in the list (e.g., change cereal):

```
shoppingList[3] = "chocolate"
```

You would end up with something like this:

Let's look at a program. Open the file list1.py. Here, we've created a list and initialized it with some data.

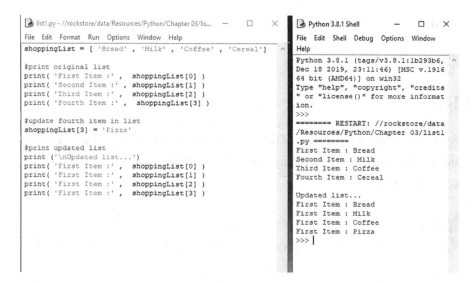

We can output data from the list using a print statement and a reference to the item in the shopping list:

```
print (shoppingList[3])
```

We can also update an item in the list using the reference:

```
shoppingList[3] = 'pizza'
```

Two-Dimensional Lists

Two-dimensional lists are visualized as a grid similar to a table with rows and columns. Each column in the grid is numbered starting with 0. Similarly, each row is numbered starting with 0. Each cell in the grid is identified by an index – the row index followed by the column index (shown in the circles).

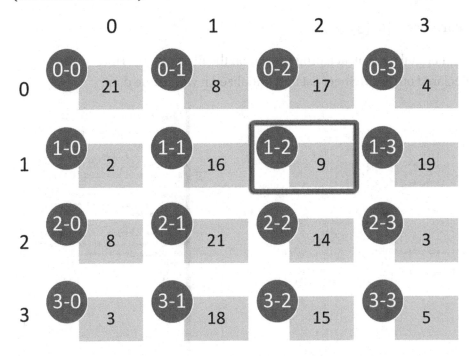

You could declare the earlier list as

```
scoreSheet = [
    [ 21, 8, 17, 4 ],
    [ 2, 16, 9, 19 ],
    [ 8, 21, 14, 3 ],
    [ 3, 18, 15, 5 ]
]
```

To reference an item in a two-dimensional list, put both the references in square brackets (first the row index, then the column index):

```
print (scoreSheet[1][2]) #circled above
```

You can change items in the list, put both the references in square brackets (first the row index, then the column index), and then assign the value:

```
scoreSheet [0][3] = 21
```

Let's take a look at a program. Open the file list2d.py. Here, we've declared our shoreSheet list and initialized it with some data.

```
scoreSheet = [
    [ 21, 8, 17, 4 ],
    [ 2, 16, 9, 19 ],
    [ 8, 21, 14, 3 ],
    [ 3, 18, 15, 5 ]
]

#print original list
print( 'Item :' ,  scoreSheet[1][2] )

#change item [1][2] in grid to 21
scoreSheet[1][2] = 21

#print original list
print( 'Item :' ,  scoreSheet[1][2] )
```

```
Python 3.8.1 (tags/v3.8.1:1b29
3b6, Dec 18 2019, 23:11:46) [M
SC v.1916 64 bit (AMD64)] on w
in32
Type "help", "copyright", "cre
dits" or "license()" for more
information.
>>>
======== RESTART: //rockstore/
data/Resources/Python/Chapter
03/list2d.py =======
Item : 9
Item : 21
>>>
```

We can add an item to a particular location in the list:

```
scoreSheet [1][2] = 21
```

We can also output data stored at a particular location:

```
print (scoreSheet[1][2])
```

Sets

A set is an unordered collection of unique items enclosed in curly braces { }. Sets can contain different types.

You can create a set like this:

```
setName = {1, 6, 2, 9}
```

Two things to note about sets. Firstly, you can't index individual elements in the set as it is an unordered data type. Secondly, you can't change individual values in the set like you can with lists. However, you can add or remove items. Use the .add()method, and type the data to add, in the parentheses.

```
setName.add('item to add')
```

Let's take a look at a program. Open the file sets.py. Here, we've created a set with some animal names. We can output the data in the set.

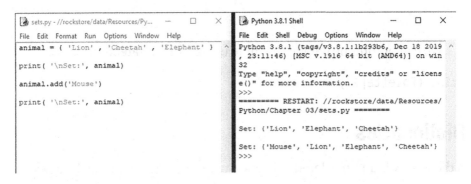

We can also add an item to the set using the .add() method.

Tuples

A tuple is similar to a list and is a sequence of items each identified by an index. As with lists, the index starts with 0 not 1.

In contrast to lists, items in a tuple can't be changed once assigned, and tuples can contain different types of data.

To create a tuple, enclose the items inside parentheses ( ):

```
userDetails = (1, 'John', '123 May Road')
```

Use a tuple when you want to store a data of a different type, such a sign in details for your website.

Let's take a look at a program. Open the file tuple.py. Here, we've created a tuple with some colors.

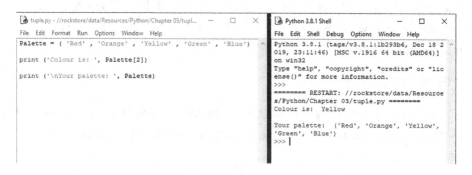

We can output the data in the tuple using a print statement:

```
print (Palette[2])
```

Dictionaries

A dictionary is an unordered collection of items, each identified by a key.

To create a dictionary, enclose the items inside braces { }. Identify each item with a key using a colon.

```
dictionary = { 1: 'Dave',
               2: 'Jo'
               3: 'Jane'
}
```

To read a value, put the key in square brackets:

```
print (dictionary[1])
```

To change or add a value, put the key in square brackets. For example, change "jo" to "mike."

```
dictionary[2] = 'Mike'
```

Let's take a look at a program. Open the file dictionary.py. Here, we've created a dictionary with some user data.

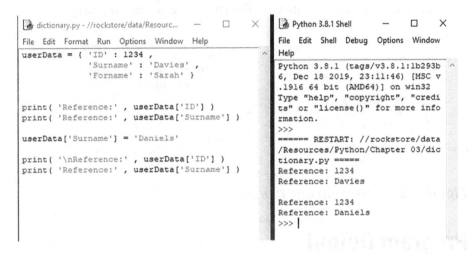

We can reference the data using the key, for example, "ID":

```
print (userData['ID'])
```

Program Input

One of the main reasons for writing a program is so you can run it multiple times with various different data.

39

Instead of hard coding the input data into a variable as we've done previously, it would be better to prompt the user for the input or retrieve it from a file (see later).

Instead of writing

```
a = 7
```

we can use the **input()** function to prompt the user for a number:

```
a = input ('Enter a number: ')
```

It's a good idea to separate your data from the actual program.

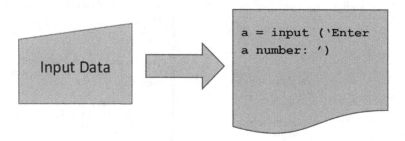

Figure 3-2. *Input data into a program*

Program Output

Any result calculated by the program needs to be displayed to the user in a meaningful way. We can either output the data to the screen using the print() function, or we can write the data to a file (see later).

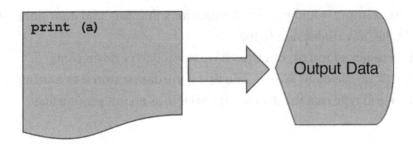

Figure 3-3. *Data output from program*

Casting Data Types

Variables can contain various types of data such as text (called a string), a whole number (called an integer), or a floating point number (numbers with decimal points).

With Python, you don't have to declare all your variables before you use them. However, you might need to convert variables to different types. This is known as type casting.

Python has two types of type conversion: implicit and explicit.

With implicit type conversion, Python automatically converts one data type to another.

With explicit type conversion, the programmer converts the data type to the required data type using a specific function. You can use the following functions to cast your data types:

int( ) converts data to an integer

long( ) converts data to a long integer

float( ) converts data to a floating point number

str( ) converts data to a string

For example, we use the **input( )** function to prompt the user for some data:

```
a = input ('Enter first number: ')
```

This example would prompt the user for some data and then store the data in the "a" variable as a string.

This might sound ok, but what if we wanted to perform some arithmetic on the data? We can't do that if the data is stored as a string. We'd have to type cast the data in the variable as an integer or a float.

```
int(a)
```

or

```
float(a)
```

Arithmetic Operators

Within the Python language, there are some arithmetic operators you can use.

Operator	Description
**	Power, indices
/	Divide
*	Multiply
+	Add
-	Subtract

Operator Precedence

BIDMAS (sometimes called BODMAS) is an acronym commonly used to remember mathematical operator precedence – that is, the order in which you evaluate each operator:

1. Brackets ( )

2. Indices (sqrt, power, squared^2, cubed^3, etc.) **

3. Divide /

4.   Multiply *

5.   Add +

6.   Subtract -

Performing Arithmetic

If you wanted to add 20% sales tax to a price of £12.95, you could do something like this:

```
total = 12.95 + 12.95 * 20 / 100
```

According to the precedence list given earlier, you would first evaluate the "divide" operator:

```
20 / 100 = 0.2
```

Next is multiply:

```
12.95 * 0.2 = 2.59
```

Finally addition:

```
12.95 + 2.59 = 15.54
```

Comparison Operators

These are used to compare values and are commonly used in conditional statements or constructing loops.

Operator	Description
==	Equal to
!=	Not equal to
>	Greater that
<	Less that
>=	Greater than or equal to
<=	Less than or equal to

For example, comparing two values in an "if" statement, you could write something like this:

```
if a > 10:
    print ("You've gone over 10...")
```

Boolean Operators

Also known as logical operators and are commonly used in conditional statements (if…) or constructing loops (while… for…).

Operator	Description
and	Returns true if both the operands are true
or	Returns true if either of the operands is true
not	Returns true if operand is false

For example, you could join two comparisons in an "if" statement using "and," like this:

```
if a >= 0 and a <= 10:
    print ("Your number is between 0 and 10")
else
    print ("Out of range - must be between 0 & 10")
Using the 'and' operator would mean both conditions
(a >= 0) and
(a <= 10) must be true.
```

Bitwise Operators

Bitwise operators are used to compare binary numbers:

Operator	Name	Description
&	AND	Sets each bit to 1 if both bits are 1
|	OR	Sets each bit to 1 if one of two bits is 1
^	XOR	Sets each bit to 1 if only one of two bits is 1
~	NOT	Inverts all the bits
<<	Left shift	Shift bits to the left
>>	Right shift	Shift bits to the right

You can apply the bitwise operators:

```
a >> 2 #shift bits of 'a' left by 2 units
a << 2 #shift bits of 'a' right by 2 units
a & b #perform AND operation on bits
```

Lab Exercises

Write a program that accepts a length in inches and prints the length in centimeters (1 inch = 2.54cm).

Write a program that accepts your forename, surname, and year of birth and adds them to an array.

Write a program that converts temperatures from Celsius to Fahrenheit:

```
F = C × 9/5 + 32
```

Write a program that calculates the volume of a sphere:

$$V = 4/3 \ \pi r^3$$

Write a program to calculate and display an employee's gross and net pay. In this scenario, tax is deducted from the gross pay at a rate of 20% to give the net pay.

Write a program that stores a shopping list of ten items. Print the whole list to the screen, and then print items 2 and 8.

Extend the previous program, to insert an item into the list.

What is a Boolean operator? Write a program to demonstrate.

What is a comparison operator? Write a program to demonstrate.

What is data type casting? Why do we need it? Write a program to demonstrate.

Summary

- A variable is a labeled location in memory that is used to store values within a computer program

- Variables defined within a function are called local variables, as they are local to that particular function.

- Global variables are defined in the main body of the program outside any particular functions.

- An integer is a whole number and can be positive or negative. Integers can usually be of unlimited length.

- A floating point number, sometimes called a real number, is a number that has a decimal point.

- A string must be enclosed in quotes.

- A list is an ordered sequence of data items usually of the same type, each identified by an index.

- A set is an unordered collection of unique items enclosed in curly braces.

- A tuple is similar to a list and is a sequence of items each identified by an index. Items in a tuple can't be changed once assigned and tuples can contain different types of data.

- A dictionary is an unordered collection of items, each identified by a key.

- We can use the input() function to prompt the user for a number.

- Converting variables to different types is known as type casting.

CHAPTER 4

Flow Control

Flow control is controlling the order in which statements or function calls of a program are executed.

There are three control structures: sequence, selection, and iteration.

Python has various control structures such as while loops, for loops, and if statements, which are used to determine which section of code is executed according to certain conditions.

Sequence

A computer program is a set of step-by-step instructions that are carried out in sequence to achieve a task or solve a problem. The sequence can contain any number of instructions, but no instruction can be skipped in the sequence. Figure 4-1 illustrates this.

© Kevin Wilson 2022

K. Wilson, *The Absolute Beginner's Guide to Python Programming*,
https://doi.org/10.1007/978-1-4842-8716-3_4

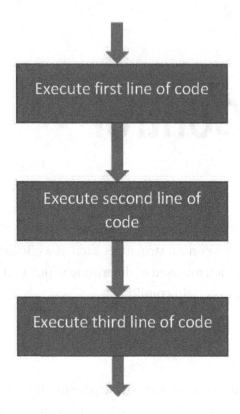

Figure 4-1. *A computer program's step-by-step sequence*

The interpreter will follow and execute each line of code in sequence until the end of the program.

Let's have a look at a program. Open adder.py. This program has four statements.

Once you execute the program, the instructions are carried out in sequence.

Let's try another example. Open inchestocm.py.

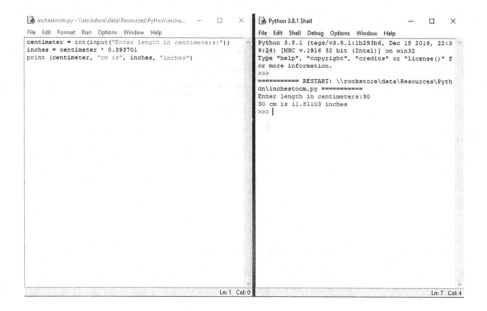

Selection

In most computer programs, there are certain points where a decision must be made. This decision is based on a condition, and that condition can be either true or false.

if... else

If statements are used if a decision is to be made. If the condition is true, then the if statement will execute the first block of code; if the condition is false, the if statement will execute the "else" block of code if included.

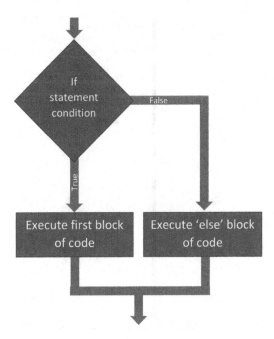

Figure 4-2. *An if... else statement*

So, for example:

```
if num >= 0: #condition
    print("Positive or Zero") #first block
else:
    print("Negative number") #else block
```

Let's have a look at a program. Open selection.py. Here, we can see a very simple if statement to determine whether a test score is a pass or fail. The pass mark is 70, so we need an if statement to return a pass message if the value entered is greater than 70. Remember that we also need to cast the variable "mark" as an integer (int).

If you enter a value greater than 70, the Python interpreter will execute the first block of the "if statement."

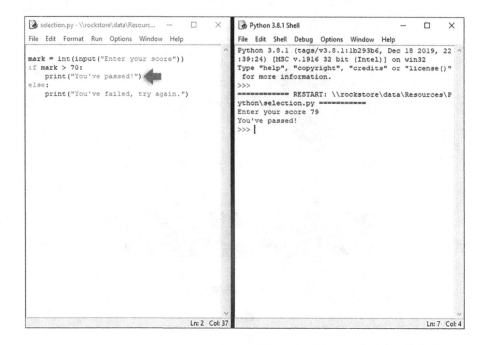

If you enter a value below 70, the Python interpreter will execute the "else block" of the "if statement."

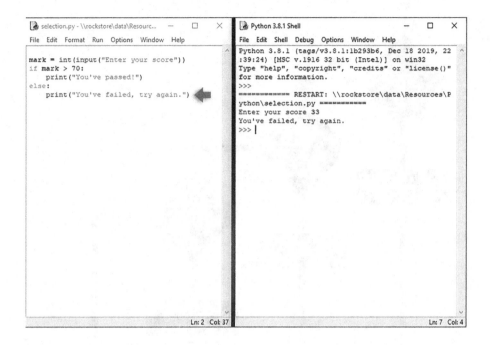

elif

Use the `elif` statement if multiple decisions are to be made. Each decision (or condition) will have a set of instructions to be executed.

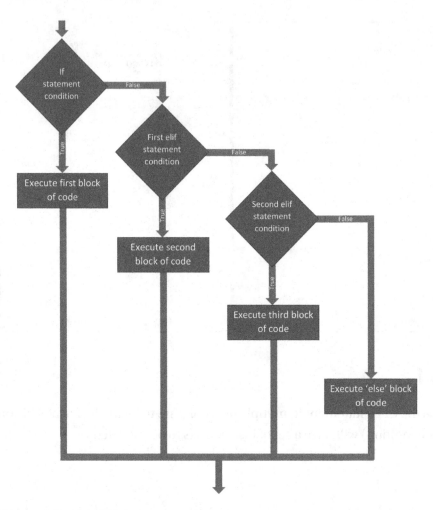

Figure 4-3. *An elif statement*

So, for example:

```
if condition:      #if condition
    [statements]    #first block of code
elif condition:  #first elif statement
    [statements]    #second block of code
elif condition:  #second elif statement
    [statements]    #third block of code
```

```
else:
    [statements] #else block of code
```

Let's have a look at a program. Open multiselection.py.

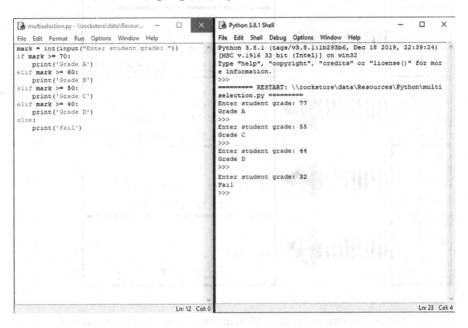

If we analyze the elif statement, we can see how it works. For the first condition, any number entered above 70 will execute the first block.

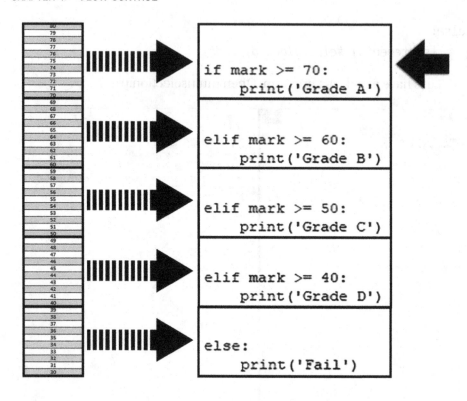

Any number between 60 and 69, the interpreter will execute the
second block.

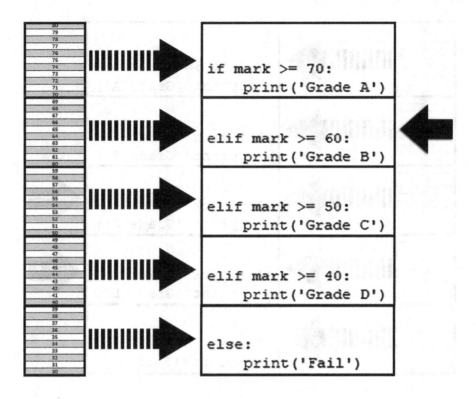

Similarly for the other conditions, 50–59 and 40–49.

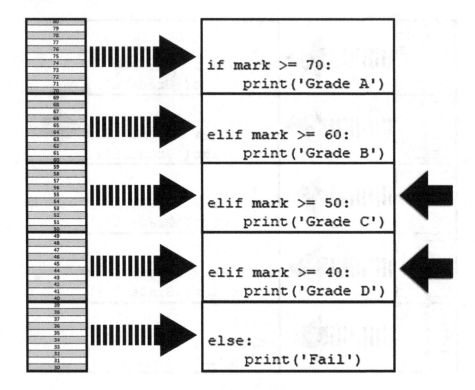

If any condition is not met by the above "elif" statements, the interpreter will execute the "else" block at the end.

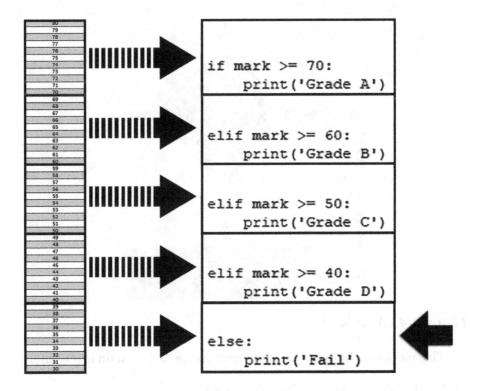

Iteration (Loops)

A loop is a set of statements that are repeated until a specific condition is met. We will look at two types of loops: the for loop and the while loop.

For Loop

A for loop executes a set of statements for each item in a sequence such as a list or string or a range. It allows a code block to be repeated a specific number of times.

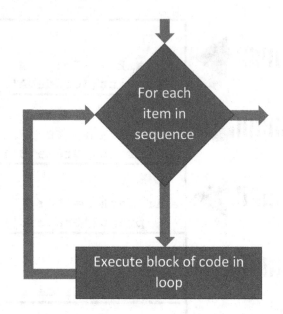

Figure 4-4. *A for loop*

This particular loop will print out each name in the list on a new line:

```
list = ['john', 'lucy', 'kate', 'mike']
for val in list:
    print (val) #block of code in loop
```

Let's have a look at a program. Open forloop.py. The for loop contains a loop condition. In this example, the loop will execute for each item in the fruitlist [sequence].

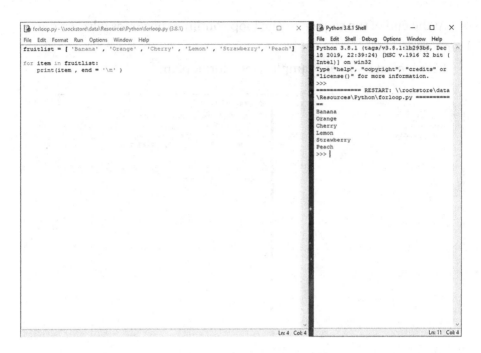

The "item" variable in the "for loop" statement is a pointer or counter to the current value or item in the sequence.

```
fruitlist = [ 'Banana' , 'Orange' , 'Cherry' , 'Lemon' , 'Strawberry', 'Peach']
```

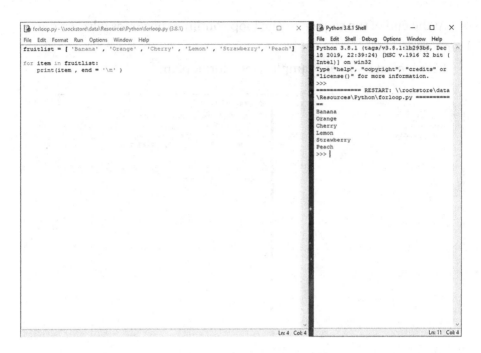

item

For each of these "items," the interpreter will execute everything inside the loop, in this example the "print" statement:

```
print (item, end='\n')
```

The interpreter will test the condition in the for loop again, and if it is true, the interpreter will execute everything inside the loop again. In each iteration of the loop, the counter moves to the next value or item.

```
fruitlist = [ 'Banana' , 'Orange' , 'Cherry' , 'Lemon' , 'Strawberry', 'Peach']
```

item

At the end of the sequence, the loop condition becomes false, so the loop terminates.

Let's look at another example. Open forloop2.py.

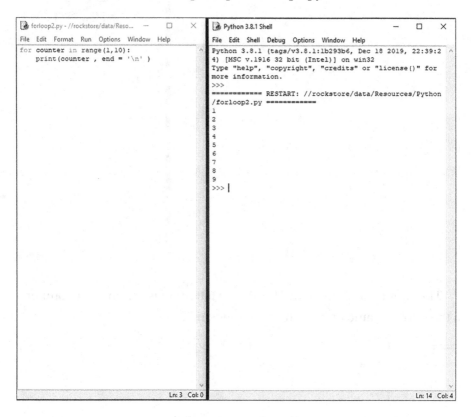

When you run through the program, you can see what it's doing.

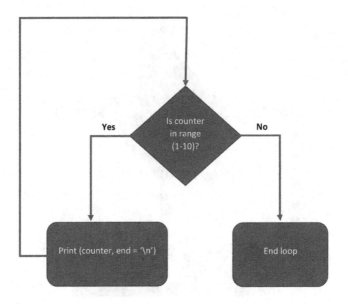

While Loop

A while loop executes a set of statements while a certain condition is true. It allows the set of statements in the code block to be repeated an unknown number of times and will continue to repeat while the condition is true.

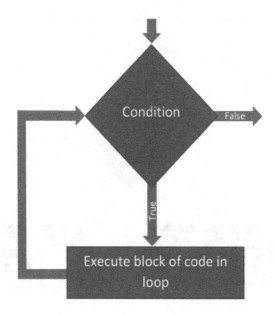

Figure 4-5. *A while loop*

This particular loop will keep prompting the user for a string until the user enters the word "fire":

```
userInput = ''
while userInput != 'fire':
    userInput = input ('Enter passcode: ')
```

Let's have a look at a program. Open whileloop.py. The while loop contains a loop condition.

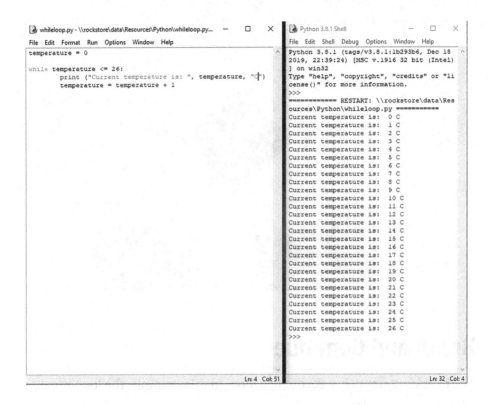

When you run through the program, you can see what it's doing:

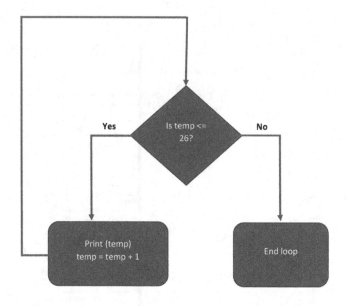

Break and Continue

The break statement breaks out of a loop. In this example, the loop breaks when the counter is equal to 5.

```
while (counter < 10):
    if counter == 5:
        break
    counter = counter + 1
```

The continue statement jumps back to the top of the loop without executing the rest of the code after the continue keyword. In this example, the loop restarts when "number" is even.

```
myList = [1, 2, 3, 4, 5, 6, 7, 8]
for number in myList:
    if number % 2 == 0: #if number even
        continue
    print(number)
```

Lab Exercises

Take a look at the following exercises and use what you've learned to solve the problems.

1. Write a program to print the numbers 1–10 to the screen.

2. Write a program to print a list of names to the screen.

3. Write a program to calculate and print the squares of the numbers from 1 to 10. Use tabs to display them in a table.

4. Write a program that accepts a number from the user until a negative number is entered.

5. Write a program that accepts an integer and prints the specified range it belongs to:

   Range 1: 0 to 10
   Range 2: 11 to 20
   Range 3: 21 to 30
   Range 4: 31 to 40

Summary

- Flow control is controlling the order in which statements or function calls of a program are executed.

- Sequence is the set of step-by-step instructions carried out in order to achieve a task or solve a problem.

- Selection is the point at which a decision is to be made. For this, we use IF statements.

- Iteration is where we need to repeat several lines of code multiple times. For this, we use WHILE and FOR loops.

- Use FOR loop if you know how many times you're going to execute the loop, such as processing a range or list.

- If you need to repeat code until a condition is to be met, use a WHILE loop.

- The break statement breaks out of a loop.

CHAPTER 5

Handling Files

Since the computer's memory (RAM) is volatile, it loses any stored data when the power is turned off. So any data that needs to be stored permanently must be saved in a file.

A file is a named location on a disk drive that is used to store data. Each file is identified by its filename.

Python contains inbuilt functions for reading data from files, as well as creating and writing to files.

In this chapter, we'll take a look at how to open files, how to read from a file, and how to write to a file.

We'll take a look at the difference between text files and binary files, as well as random access.

File Types

There are two types of files: text files and binary files. By default, Python reads and writes data in a text file.

Text File

A text file stores sequences of characters: plain text files, HTML files, and program source code.

© Kevin Wilson 2022
K. Wilson, *The Absolute Beginner's Guide to Python Programming*,
https://doi.org/10.1007/978-1-4842-8716-3_5

Use these file modes when opening a file in text mode:

- "r" opens a file for reading, error if the file does not exist.

- "a" opens a file for appending, creates the file if it does not exist.

- "w" opens a file for writing, creates the file if it does not exist.

- "r+" opens a file for both reading and writing.

Binary

A binary file is stored in the same format as the computer's memory (RAM): any images such as jpeg, audio, or program executable files.

Use these file modes when opening a file in binary mode:

- "rb" opens a file for binary reading, error if the file does not exist.

- "ab" opens a file for binary appending, creates the file if it does not exist.

- "wb" opens a file for writing, creates the file if it does not exist.

- "rb+" opens a file for both reading and writing.

Text File Operations

By default, Python opens files as text files. Text files contain readable characters as shown in the following example:

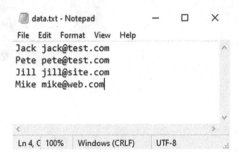

Figure 5-1. *Example of a text file*

Open Files

To open a file, use the open( ) method:

```
file = open('filename.txt', 'file mode')
```

When you open a file, put the filename and the file mode in the parameters of the open( ) method.

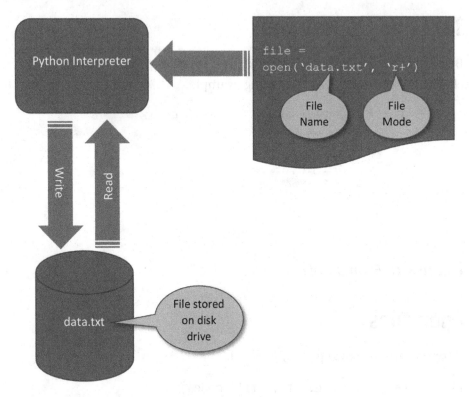

Figure 5-2. *How a file is accessed in Python*

The file mode tells the Python interpreter what you intend to do with the file, that is, read, write, or append:

- "r" opens a file for reading, error if the file does not exist.

- "a" opens a file for appending, creates the file if it does not exist.

- "w" opens a file for writing, creates the file if it does not exist.

- "r+" opens a file for both reading and writing.

This depends on the purpose of your program. It's good practice to open your file, perform your operations, and then close the file.

Write to a File

To write data to a file, use the .write( ) method:

```
file.write("Data to write to the file...")
```

When opening a file for writing, use either of the following:

- "a" opens a file for appending, creates the file if it does not exist. Adds new data to the end of file.

- "w" opens a file for writing, creates the file if it does not exist. Overwrites any existing data in file.

Let's take a look at a program. Open file.py.

```
file.py - \\rockstore\data\Resources\Python\file.py (3.8...    —    □    ×

File   Edit   Format   Run   Options   Window   Help
#get some information
username = input('Enter your name: ')
useremail = input('Enter your email: ')


#open file for writing
file = open( 'data.txt' , 'w' )


#write the data to the file data.txt
file.write (username)
file.write (' ') #add space between
file.write (useremail)


#close the file
file.close()
```

Here, we get some information from the user (a username and an email address):

```
username = input('Enter your name: ')
useremail = input('Enter your email: ')
```

Next, we open a file called "data.txt" for writing and assign it to an object called "file."

```
file = open('data.txt', 'w')
```

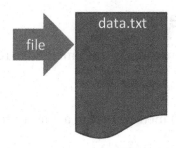

We then write the username and email address to the file using the file object's `.write` method.

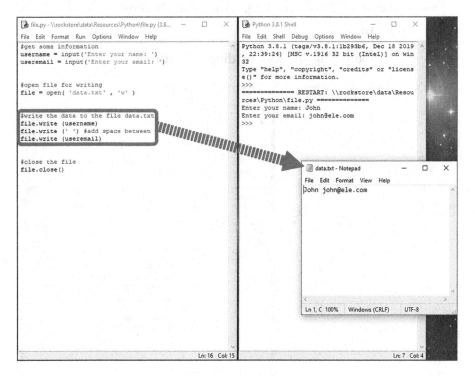

Now remember, the 'w' file mode opens a file for writing. This also means any new data will overwrite any data already stored in the file.

After we've completed our file operations, we close the file:

```
file.close()
```

Read from a File

To read data from a file, use the `.read()` method to read the whole file:

```
fileContent = fileName.read( )
```

Use the `.readline()` method to read a line at a time:

```
nextLine = fileName.readline( )
```

When opening a file for writing, use either of the following:

- "r" opens a file for reading, error if the file does not exist.

- "r+" opens a file for both reading and writing.

Let's take a look at a program. Open fileread.py.

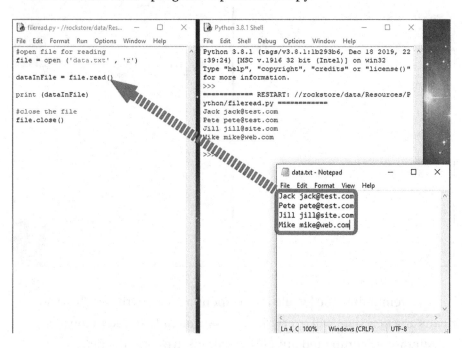

Here, we open a file called "data.txt" and assign it to an object called "file."

Next, we read the data using the "file" object's .read method and finally close the file.

Binary File Operations

Most digital data is stored in binary files as they are much smaller and faster than text files.

Binary files are not readable by humans as shown in the following example.

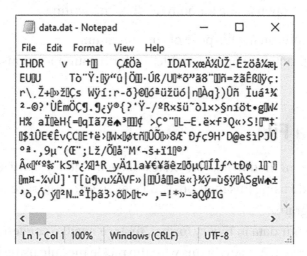

Figure 5-3. *Example of a binary file*

Open Files

To open a file, use the open() method:

```
file = open('filename.dat', 'file mode')
```

When you open a file, put the filename and the file mode in the parameters of the open()method.

The file mode tells the Python interpreter what you intend to do with the file, that is, read, write, or append:

- "rb" opens a file for reading, error if the file does not exist.

- "ab" opens a file for appending, creates the file if it does not exist.

- "wb" opens a file for writing, creates the file if it does not exist.

- "rb+" opens a file for both reading and writing.

This depends on the purpose of your program.

It's good practice to open your file, perform your operations, and then close the file.

Write to a File

The .write() method writes data in text format, and if you try to write data in binary mode using this method, you'll get an error message when you run your program.

To write your data in binary format, first we need to convert it to a sequence of bytes. We can do this with the pickle module using a process called pickling. Pickling is the process where data objects such as integers, strings, lists, and dictionaries are converted into a byte stream.

To write to a file, use the pickle.dump() method:

```
pickle.dump (data-to-be-written, file-to-write-to)
```

Let's take a look at a program. Open filewritebin.py. First, we need to include the pickle module. You can do this by using an import command.

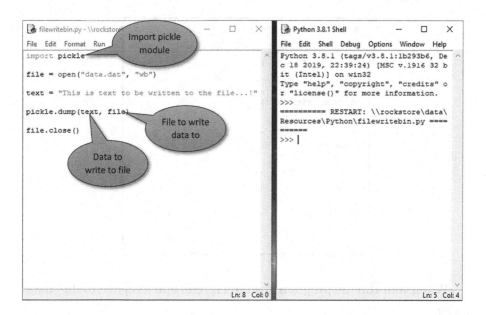

Next, we open a file in the usual way, except we set the file mode to binary write (wb).

Now, to write the data to the file, we pickle the "text" object using the `pickle.dump()` method and finally close the file.

Read a File

Remember when we wrote our data to our binary file, we used a process called pickling. Well, to read the data from the file, we use a similar process.

To read a file, use the `pickle.read()` method:

```
pickle.read (file-to-read-from)
```

Let's take a look at a program. Open filereadbin.py. First, we need to include the pickle module. You can do this using an import command.

When your run the program, the data is read and assigned to the "data" variable.

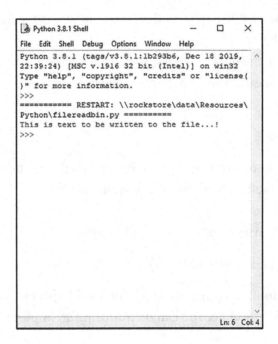

Random File Access

When a file is opened, the Python interpreter allocates a pointer within the file. This pointer determines the position in the file from where reading or writing will take place. The pointer can be moved to any location in the file.

To move the file pointer, use the `.seek()` method:

```
file.seek(position-in-file, whence)
```

The first parameter (position-in-file) determines how many bytes to move. A positive value will move the pointer forward; a negative value will move the pointer backward. The position in the file is called an offset. In a file, each position could contain one byte or one character. Remember, the numbering system starts with 0.

Using our text file as an example `file.seek(5)` would move the file pointer to the sixth byte:

```
                                012345

            Jack   jack@test.com

            Pete   pete@test.com

            Jill   jill@site.com

            Mike   mike@web.com
```

The second parameter (whence) determines where in the file to start from and accepts one of the three values:

0 – Sets the start point to the beginning of the file (the default)

1 – Sets the start point to the current position

2 – Sets the start point to the end of the file

To find the current position of the file pointer in the file, use the `.tell()` method:

```
file.tell()
```

Let's take a look at a program. Here, we're going to start reading the first line of the data.txt file starting from the sixth byte or character.

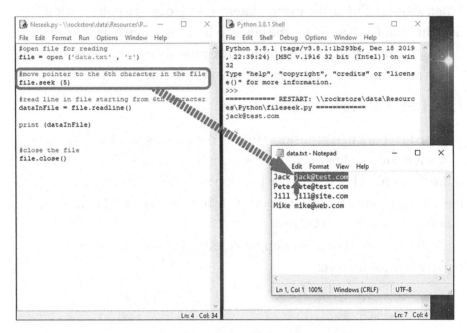

Lab Exercises

Take a look at the following exercises and use what you've learned to solve the problems.

1. Write a program that gets a string from the user and then writes it to a file along with the user's name.

2. Modify the program from exercise 1 so that it appends the data to the file rather than overwriting.

3. Write a program to write a list of names to a file.

4. Write a program to read a file line by line and store it in a list.

5. What is the difference between a text file and a binary file?

Summary

- A file is a named location on a disk drive that is used to store data. Each file is identified by its filename.

- There are two types of files: text files and binary files. By default, Python reads and writes data in a text file.

- A text file stores sequences of characters.

- A binary file is stored in the same format as the computer's memory (RAM).

- Use the open( ) method to open a file.

- To write data to a file, use the .write( ) method.

- To read data from a file, use the .read() method to read the whole file.

- To write to a binary file, first we need to convert it to a sequence of bytes. This is called pickling.

CHAPTER 6

Using Functions

Functions help break a program into smaller pieces. This avoids repetition of code, making larger programs more efficient and easier to maintain.

A function is a block of code that is only executed when called within a program.

You can pass data to the function. This data is known as a parameter or argument.

Arguments or parameters are specified inside parentheses after the function name, for example:

```
functionName(parameters)
```

A function can return data as a result.

Declaring Functions

You can declare a new function using the def keyword followed by the function name:

```
def functionName(parameters):
    code to be executed in function
```

If the function takes parameters, you can include these in parenthesis next to the function name.

© Kevin Wilson 2022

K. Wilson, *The Absolute Beginner's Guide to Python Programming*,
https://doi.org/10.1007/978-1-4842-8716-3_6

So, for example, if we wrote a function to add two numbers together, we could write something like this:

```
def addNum(num_1, num_2):
    return num_1 + num_2
```

This function takes two numbers as parameters, adds them together, and returns the result.

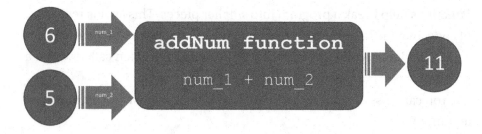

You can call the function like this:

```
result = addNum(6, 5)
```

For smaller programs, you can declare your functions in the same file – usually at the top, but as programs become larger and more complex, you should declare your functions in a separate file and then include the file in your main script. This allows you to modularize and reuse code – it is good programming practice for larger projects.

We can declare our addNum function in our myfunctions.py file and include it in our functionsmain.py file. To include functions in another script, use the import keyword:

```
import myfunctions
```

Let's have a look at a program. Open functions.py. Here, at the top of the script, we've defined a simple function to add two numbers together.

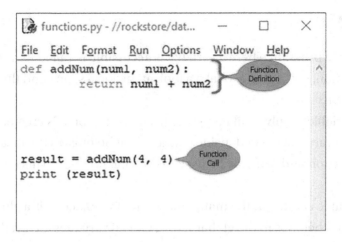

At the bottom of the script, we call our function addNum and pass two values (4, 4). We use the "return" keyword to return the result.

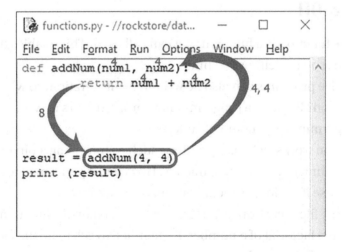

The result from the function is then assigned to the variable "result." Finally, we print the contents of the variable "result" to the screen, so we can see what is happening.

Scope

The part of a program where a variable is accessible is called its scope. In this section, we're going to take a look at the local scope and the global scope.

If a variable is only available from inside the region it is created, for example, a variable created inside a function, it belongs to the local scope of that function and can only be used inside that function. This is called local scope.

A variable created in the main body of the Python code is a global variable and belongs to the global scope. Global variables are available from within any scope, global and local.

Recursion

A recursive function is a function that can call itself. This enables the function to repeat itself several times.

Recursive programs can also be written using iteration, so why bother with recursion? Recursive programs allow programmers to write efficient code using a minimal amount of code.

Recursion works well for algorithms such as traversing a binary tree or a sort algorithm and generating fractals. However, if performance is vital, it is better to use iteration, as recursion can be a lot slower.

Open the file recursion1.py. Here, we have a recursive function that calculates the factorial of a number. Remember, to calculate the factorial, you multiply all the numbers from 1 to the given number.

```
def factorial(n):
    if n <= 1:
        return 1
```

```
else:
    a = n * factorial(n-1)
    return a
```

factorial(4)

When we call the factorial function and pass a positive integer, it will recursively call itself by decreasing the number by one each time.

For example, if we entered 4, the program will call factorial(3), factorial(2), and factorial(1).

Each time the factorial function is called, it pushes another entry onto the call stack.

The recursion ends when the number reduces to 1. This is called the base condition.

When the functions return, each call is popped off the stack and evaluated.

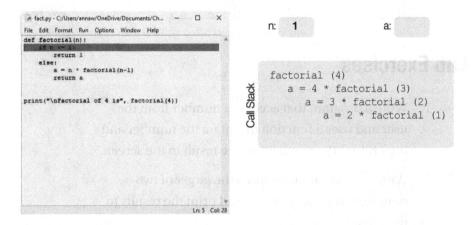

Figure 6-1. *An example of a recursive program during execution*

Here's another example, a recursive function to print out the Fibonacci numbers.

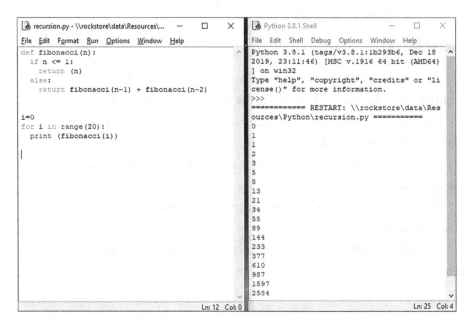

Lab Exercises

1. Write a program that accepts a number from the user and uses a function to square the number and then return the result. Print the result to the screen.

2. Write a function that returns the larger of two numbers. Test the function and print the results to the screen.

3. What is the difference between a local and a global variable?

4. What makes a function recursive?

5. Write a program that prints first ten positive numbers using a recursive function.

Summary

- Functions help break a program into smaller pieces.

- You can declare a new function using the def keyword.

- Parameters or arguments are data passed to the function.

- The part of a program where a variable is accessible is called its scope. We have taken a look at the local scope and the global scope.

- Local scope variables are only accessible to the function in which they're defined.

- Global scope variables are available anywhere.

- A recursive function is a function that can call itself.

CHAPTER 7

Using Modules

When developing more complex Python applications, as the program grows in size, it's a good idea to split it up into several files for easier maintenance and reusability of the code. To do this, we use modules.

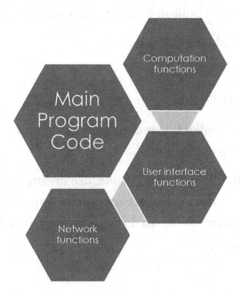

Figure 7-1. *An example of how a large program can be broken down into modules*

© Kevin Wilson 2022
K. Wilson, *The Absolute Beginner's Guide to Python Programming*,
https://doi.org/10.1007/978-1-4842-8716-3_7

Modules are simply files with the .py extension, containing code that can be imported into another program.

In doing this, we can build up a code library that contains a set of functions that you want to include when developing larger applications.

In this section, we'll take a look at how to create modules and include them in our Python programs.

Importing Modules

Python has a whole library of modules you can import into your programs. Here are some common built-in modules you can use:

> **math** – Mathematical functions
>
> **turtle** – Turtle graphics
>
> **tkinter** – GUI interface toolkit
>
> **pygame** – Toolkit for creating games and other multimedia applications.

To import the modules into your code, use the import keyword. In this example, I'm going to use the import keyword to import the turtle graphics module into a Python program. To do this, we enter the following line at the top of the program:

```
import turtle
```

This statement imports all the turtle graphics functions into the program.

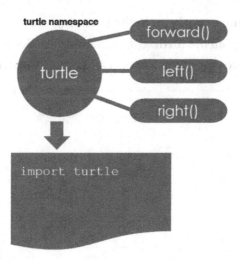

Figure 7-2. *How to import a module into a program*

Turtle graphics operate much like a drawing board, in which you can execute various commands to move a turtle around. We can use functions like forward() and right(). The turtle will travel along the path that you define using these functions, leaving a pen mark behind it.

When we import a module, we are making it available in our program as a separate namespace. In other words, each module has its own private namespace which usually has the same name as the module. This namespace holds all the names of functions and variables declared in that module. This means that we have to refer to the function in a particular module using the dot notation.

moduleName.functionName()

For example:

turtle.forward(100)

turtle is the name of the module we imported earlier, and forward() is a function defined within the module.

Let's put this into a program. In the following, we have our import statement to import all the turtle graphics modules. Below that, we have a statement that moves the turtle forward and one to finish the program.

Notice that we use the dot notation to access the functions in the turtle module:

```
moduleName.functionName()
```

We want to access the forward function, so we specify the module name it's in (turtle), followed by a dot, and then the name of the function we want (forward). So we get

```
turtle.forward(100)
```

This will move the turtle 100 pixels forward.

Here, we can see the output to the program: the turtle has moved 100 pixels to the right.

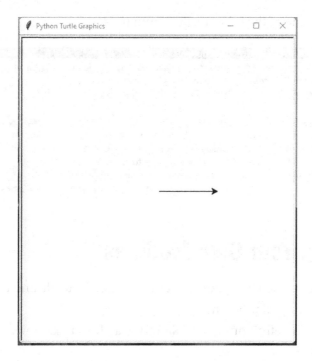

We can complete the program to draw a square.

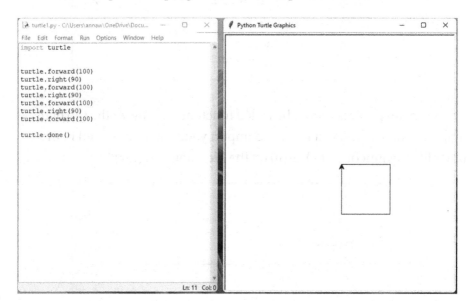

Try out some of the other turtle commands.

Command	Description
turtle.forward(distance)	Move the turtle forward by the specified distance
turtle.backward(distance)	Move the turtle backward by distance,
turtle.home()	Move turtle to the origin – coordinates (0,0)
turtle.penup()	Pull the pen up
turtle.pendown()	Pull the pen down
turtle.pencolor(colorstring)	Set pencolor to colorstring, such as "red", "yellow" etc.
turtle.circle(radius)	Draw a circle with given radius.
turtle.shape("turtle")	Sets the turtle shape to turtle.
turtle.undo()	Undo (repeatedly) the last turtle action(s)
turtle.clear()	Erases all drawings that currently appear in the graphics window.

Creating Your Own Modules

You can declare and store your functions in a separate file and import them into your main program.

All function definitions can be stored in a file, for example, myfunctions.py.

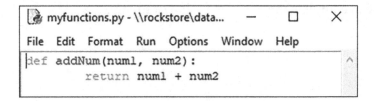

The main program could be called functionmain.py. At the top of the main program script, you'll need to import your functions stored in the other file (myfunctions.py). Strip off the file extension (.py).

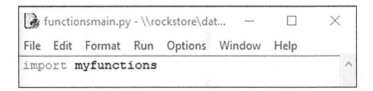

This is called a module. Any functions declared will be included in the main program. You can include these functions in any program you need to. This makes maintenance easier.

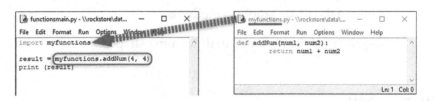

Now, to call any functions from that module, you need to specify the module name followed by the function name.

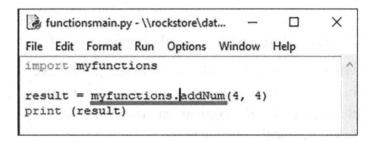

Lab Exercises

1.   Write a function that accepts a number from the user and uses a function to square the number and then return the result.

2.   Save this file as a module.

3.   Import the module you just created into a new program.

4.   Call the function in the module.

5. Create a new program and import the turtle graphics module.

6. Experiment with drawing different shapes using some of the turtle graphics methods.

7. Use the turtle commands to draw some shapes.

Summary

- Modules are simply files with the .py extension, containing code that can be imported into another program.

- You can import modules using the import keyword.

- When we import a module, we are making it available in our program as a separate namespace. This means that we have to refer to the function in a particular module using the dot notation.

CHAPTER 8

Exception Handling

An exception is an error that occurs during execution of a program, sometimes called a runtime error. This could be a "file not found" error if you are trying to load a file that doesn't exist, or a "type error" if you type text into a field when the program is expecting a number.

Exceptions are useful for handling errors encountered with file handling, network access, and data input.

These errors can be handled gracefully using Python's exception handling procedures.

Types of Exception

Here's a list of built-in exceptions according to the Python documentation.

Table 8-1. *Built in Python Exceptions*

Exception	Cause
AssertionError	Raised when assert statement fails
AttributeError	Raised when attribute assignment or reference fails
EOFError	Raised when the input() function hits end-of-file condition
FileNotFoundError	Raised when a file or directory is requested but doesn't exist. Corresponds to errno ENOENT
FloatingPointError	Raised when a floating point operation fails

(continued)

© Kevin Wilson 2022
K. Wilson, *The Absolute Beginner's Guide to Python Programming*,
https://doi.org/10.1007/978-1-4842-8716-3_8

Table 8-1. (*continued*)

Exception	Cause
GeneratorExit	Raised when a generator's close() method is called
ImportError	Raised when the imported module is not found
IndexError	Raised when index of a sequence is out of range
KeyError	Raised when a key is not found in a dictionary
KeyboardInterrupt	Raised when the user hits interrupt key (Ctrl+C or delete)
MemoryError	Raised when an operation runs out of memory
NameError	Raised when a variable is not found in local or global scope
NotImplementedError	Raised by abstract methods
OSError	Raised when system operation causes system-related error
OverflowError	Raised when result of an arithmetic operation is too large to be represented
ReferenceError	Raised when a weak reference proxy is used to access a garbage collected referent
RuntimeError	Raised when an error does not fall under any other category
StopIteration	Raised by next() function to indicate that there is no further item to be returned by iterator
SyntaxError	Raised by parser when syntax error is encountered
IndentationError	Raised when there is incorrect indentation
TabError	Raised when indentation consists of inconsistent tabs and spaces
SystemError	Raised when interpreter detects internal error
SystemExit	Raised by sys.exit() function

(*continued*)

Table 8-1. (*continued*)

Exception	Cause
TypeError	Raised when a function or operation is applied to an object of incorrect type
UnboundLocalError	Raised when a reference is made to a local variable in a function or method, but no value has been bound to that variable
UnicodeError	Raised when a Unicode-related encoding or decoding error occurs
UnicodeEncodeError	Raised when a Unicode-related error occurs during encoding
UnicodeDecodeError	Raised when a Unicode-related error occurs during decoding
UnicodeTranslateError	Raised when a Unicode-related error occurs during translating
ValueError	Raised when a function gets argument of correct type but improper value
ZeroDivisionError	Raised when second operand of division or modulo operation is zero

Whenever an exception occurs, the interpreter halts the execution of the program and raises an exception error as shown in the table.

You can catch these exceptions using the `try` and `except` keywords and provide code to handle the error.

Catching Exceptions

If we run the following code, the Python interpreter will raise a `FileNotFoundError` exception because there is no file called "file.txt". This will cause the program to crash.

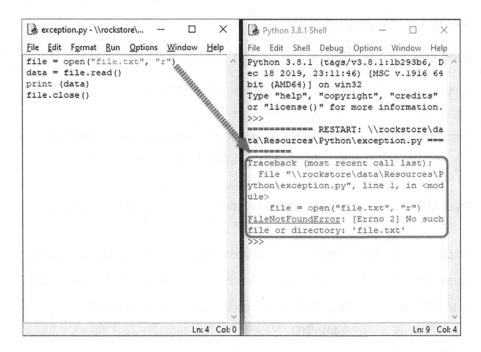

You can catch exceptions using the try and except keywords. Just put your code in the "try" block and your error handling code for each exception in the "exception" block as shown here:

```
try:
    # Code to execute as normal
except [exception (see table above)]:
    # Code to deal with exception
```

The try block contains the code to execute. The except block contains the code to handle the error.

Let's take a look at the program again. We can take our code and place it in the "try'" block. Then add an "except" block to deal with the error. If we look at the error message in the shell, we see this is a FileNotFoundError. We can add this after the "except" keyword.

Now, when we run the program, we get a simple message rather than an ugly error.

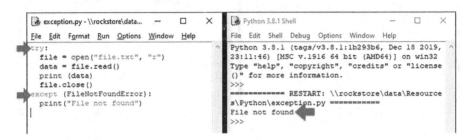

Use the `finally` block to perform any clean up. The `finally` statement runs regardless of whether the `try` statement produces an exception or not.

```
try:
    file = open("file.txt", "r") data = file.read()
except FileNotFoundError: print("File not found")
    finally: f.close()
```

Raising Your Own Exceptions

Use the `raise` keyword to force a specified exception to occur followed by the type of error using the table in Table 8-1 at the beginning of this chapter.

```
if number < 0:
    raise ValueError ("Negative numbers only.")
```

Here in the file raise.py, we've raised a ValueError exception.

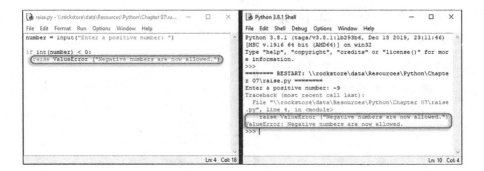

Summary

- An exception is an error that occurs during execution of a program, sometimes called a runtime error.

- You can catch exceptions using the **try** and **except** keywords.

CHAPTER 9

Object-Oriented Programming

Python is an object-oriented programming language. This means that the program design is based around objects, rather than functions and logic.

Each object is created using a blueprint known as a class. Each class has attributes to contain the data an object needs to work with.

Each class also contains functions, called methods that perform operations on objects.

An object is an instance of a class. So, you could have a class called "car" and use it to define an object called "merc."

You'll need the source files in the directory Chapter08.

Principles of OOP

The four principles of OOP are encapsulation, inheritance, polymorphism, and abstraction.

Encapsulation

With encapsulation, you restrict access to methods and attributes within a certain class. This prevents accidental modification of data and unwanted changes to other objects.

© Kevin Wilson 2022
K. Wilson, *The Absolute Beginner's Guide to Python Programming*,
https://doi.org/10.1007/978-1-4842-8716-3_9

Inheritance

A class can inherit all the methods and attributes from another class. If a class called "person" had the attributes name, age, and dob, we could use this class to define two other child classes called "student" and "staff." Both inherit the methods and attributes from the "person" class.

Polymorphism

Polymorphism allows us to define methods in the child class with the same name as defined in the parent class. This is known as method overriding.

Polymorphism also allows us to define methods that can take many forms.

Abstraction

Abstraction is the process of reducing objects to their essence so that only the necessary elements are represented. In other words, you remove all irrelevant information about an object in order to reduce its complexity.

Classes and Objects

You can define a class using the class keyword:

```
class <class-name> :
    <class attributes and methods>
```

Here, we have created a class called Person:

```
class Person :
```

All classes have a function called init () which is automatically executed when the class is initiated. Use the init () function to initialize attributes.

```
def  init  (self, name, dob, email):
    self.name = name
    self.dob = dob
    self.email = email
```

The self keyword represents the current instance of the class (i.e., the object created from the class). By using the self keyword, you can access the attributes of the object itself.

When you declare a method, you pass the current instance of the class (i.e., the object itself), along with any other parameters required, to the method:

```
def getAge(self):
    currentDate = date.today()
    age = currentDate.year - self.dob.year
    return age
```

When you need to use any attribute, you use self followed by the attribute name:

```
self.attribute-name
```

So, for example:

```
self.email
```

Let's take a look at a program. Open the file class.py. Here, we've defined our "Person" class.

```
class.py - \\rockstore\data\Resources\Python\Chapter 08\class.py (3.8.1)    —    □    ✕

File  Edit  Format  Run  Options  Window  Help

from datetime import date

class Person :

    #define initialisations
    def __init__(self, name, dob, email):
        self.name = name
        self.dob = dob
        self.email = email

    #define class methods
    def getAge(self):
        currentDate = date.today()
        age = currentDate.year - self.dob.year
        return age
```

To create an object from the class, call the class Person(...) and pass any data using parenthesis ( ). Assign the new object to a variable, for example, person.

```
#create an object
person = Person (
        "Sophie", #name
        date(1999, 4, 2), #DOB (year, month, day)
        "Sophie@mymail.com", #email
)
```

To use the object, use the dot notation:

classname.method()

or

classname.attribute

So in our example, to use the attributes we use the dot notation, with the object name followed by the attribute name as we can see here:

```
print(person.name)
print(person.email)
```

Similarly, if we want to use the methods of an object, we use the dot notation, with the object name followed by the method name as we can see here:

```
print(person.getAge())
```

Class Inheritance

We mentioned earlier that inheritance means a class can inherit all the methods and attributes from another class.

As we can see in Figure 9-1, we have a parent or super class called Person and two child (or sub) classes called Student and Staff.

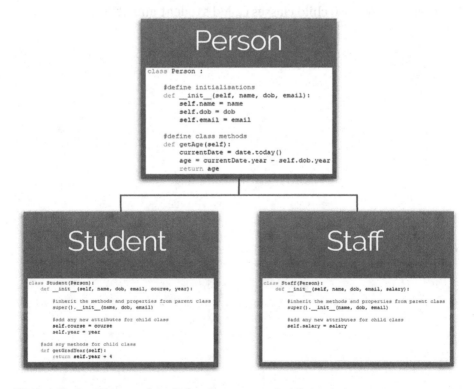

Figure 9-1. *How a class inherits properties from its parent*

The child classes inherit all the attributes and methods of the parent classes. Child classes can include any additional attributes and methods that are not accessible from other classes.

To create a child class, declare the class as normal, except include the parent class in parenthesis after the class name. So

```
class child-class(parent-class):
```

If you want to inherit all the methods and properties from the parent, use super():

```
super(). init (name, dob, email)
```

Open the file inherit.py. Here, we've created a class called person. We've also created two child classes called student and staff.

```
inherit.py - \\rockstore\data\Resources\Python\Chapter 08\inherit.py (3.8.1)        —     □     ×

File   Edit   Format   Run   Options   Window   Help

class Person :

    #define initialisations
    def __init__(self, name, dob, email):
        self.name = name
        self.dob = dob
        self.email = email

    #define class methods
    def getAge(self):
        currentDate = date.today()
        age = currentDate.year - self.dob.year
        return age

class Student(Person):
    def __init__(self, name, dob, email, course, year):

        #inherit the methods and properties from parent class
        super().__init__(name, dob, email)

        #add any new attributes for child class
        self.course = course
        self.year = year

    #add any methods for child class
    def getGradYear(self):
        return self.year + 4

class Staff(Person):
    def __init__(self, name, dob, email, salary):

        #inherit the methods and properties from parent class
        super().__init__(name, dob, email)

        #add any new attributes for child class
        self.salary = salary
```

We can create a lecturer object from the class Staff.

```
#create an object
lecturer = Staff (
        "John", #name
        date(1977, 4, 2), #DOB (year, month, day)
        "John@mymail.com", #email
        44000
)
```

115

To reference our attributes, we use the dot notation.

```
print ("\nStaff Member: ", lecturer.name)
print ("Salary: ", "£", lecturer.salary)
```

Polymorphic Classes

In this example, we're going to create two classes. To be polymorphic, each of these classes needs to have an interface in common. So we define methods for each class that have the same name. In this case, we can define a method that calculates the area in each class (triangle, square, and circle as we can see in Figure 9-2).

Figure 9-2.   *An example of how classes can contain the same method*

Open the file polyclass.py. Here, we've defined a class for triangle, square, and circle. Notice each class has a method called getArea().

```
polyclass.py - \\rockstore\data\Resources\Python\Chapter 08\polyclass.py (3....    —    □    ✕
File  Edit  Format  Run  Options  Window  Help
class Polygon:
    def __init__(self, width, height):
        self.width = width
        self.height = height

class Triangle(Polygon):
    def getArea(self):
        return self.width * self.height / 2

class Square(Polygon):
    def getArea(self):
        return self.width * self.height

class Circle:
    def __init__(self, radius):
        self.radius = radius

    def getArea(self):
        return 3.14 * self.radius ** 2
```

This means we can call the .getArea() method for each object created.

```
print(square.getArea())

print(triangle.getArea())

print(circ.getArea())
```

Method Overriding

With method overriding, you can define a method with the same name in the child class as in the parent class. The method in the child class overrides the method in its parent class.

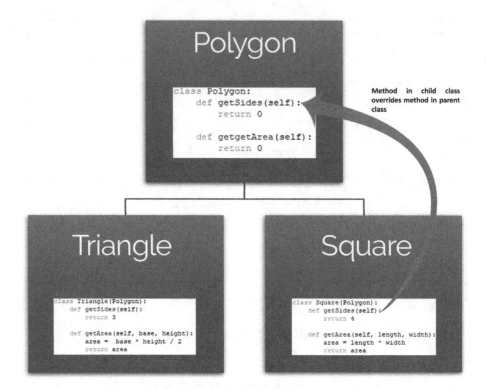

Figure 9-3. *How a method in a child class can override the method defined in the parent class*

Have a look at methodoverride.py. Here, we've defined the classes discussed earlier. The methods in the child classes have the same name as in the parent class. Each method is redefined and specific to the class. Let's see what happens when we create our objects and call the methods.

```
# Create triangle object
tri = Triangle()

# Call getArea method for triangle
print (tri.getArea(22, 22))

# Create pentagon object
pent = Pentagon()

# Call getArea method for pentagon
print (pent.getArea(22))
```

Give it a try.

Lab Exercises

1. Declare a new class called Vehicle without any attributes and methods.

2. Add some attributes to the Vehicle class such as

   Name
   Speed
   Mileage

3. Add a method to the Vehicle class to return the vehicle name.

4. Create a child class called Car that will inherit all the variables and methods of the Vehicle class.

5. Create a child class called Taxi.

6. Add a method to the Taxi class to collect the fair.

Summary

- Python is an object-oriented programming language.

- A class is a blueprint for an object.

- Each class has attributes to contain the data an object needs to work with.

- Each class contains functions, called methods that perform operations on objects.

- Encapsulation restrict access to methods and attributes within a certain class.

- A class can inherit all the methods and attributes from another class. Child classes inherit methods and attributes from the parent.

- Polymorphism allows us to define methods in the child class with the same name as defined in the parent class.

- Abstraction is the process of reducing objects to their essence so that only the necessary elements are represented.

- You can define a class using the class keyword.

- To use methods defined in an object, use the dot notation.

- Method overriding allows you to define a method with the same name in the child class as in the parent class.

CHAPTER 10

Building an Interface

Modern computer applications are built with graphical user interfaces in mind. The user interacts with the application using windows, icons, menus, and a mouse pointer rather than console-based I/O.

To create a graphical user interface using Python, you'll need to use Tkinter (Tk interface). This module is bundled with standard distributions of Python for all platforms.

Creating a Window

The first thing you need to do is import the Tkinter module into your program. To do this, use

```
from tkinter import *
```

To create a window, use the Tk() method:

```
window = Tk()
```

Add a title:

```
window.title('Window Title')
```

Set the initial size and position of the window. Use the .geometry() method.

```
window.geometry("800x600+50+20")
```

© Kevin Wilson 2022
K. Wilson, *The Absolute Beginner's Guide to Python Programming*,
https://doi.org/10.1007/978-1-4842-8716-3_10

The first two numbers, in this case "800x600," set the window size. Set this to the desired window size in pixels. This could be 1280x720, 1920x1080, and so on.

The second two numbers, in this case "50+20," set the initial position of the window on the screen using *x* and *y* coordinates.

Let's take a look at a program. Open window.py. Here, we've created a window. You can do this using the Tk() function and assign it to a window object.

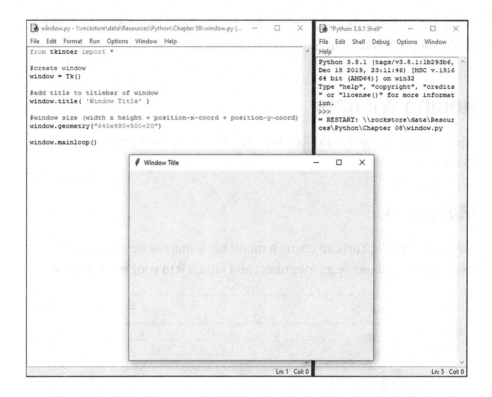

We've sized the window, so that is 640 pixels wide by 480 pixels high. We've also positioned the window 500 pixels across from the top left by 20 pixels down. You can do this using the `.geometry()` method. This is the initial size and position of the window on screen.

We've also added a window title. You can do this using the `.title()` method. This helps to identify your app.

Finally, to make the window appear, we need to enter the Tkinter event loop. You can do this with the `.mainloop()` method:

```
window.mainloop()
```

This is an infinite loop used to run the application and is called an event loop. The `.mainloop()` method waits for an event such as a keypress or mouse click events from the window system and dispatches them to the application widgets (frames, buttons, menus, etc.).

Adding Widgets

Widgets are standard items for building a graphical user interface using Tkinter.

Menus

Let's add a menu. You can create a menu bar using the Menu() function. Assign it to an object (e.g., menubar) and attach it to your main window.

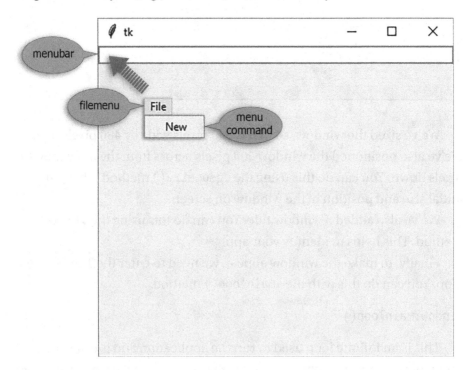

Now you need to create the individual menus (such as "file," "edit," etc.) on the menubar.

```
filemenu = Menu(menubar-to-add-to, menu-style)
```

Add the menus to the menubar:

```
menubar.add_cascade(menu-label, menu-to-add-to)
```

For each menu you create (e.g., filemenu), you need to create each menu command (such as "new," "save," "exit," etc.):

```
filemenu.add_command(command-label, function)
```

Finally, add the menubar you've created to the main window:

```
window.config(menu-to-add)
```

Let's take a look at a program. Open the file menu.py. Here, we've written the program as described earlier.

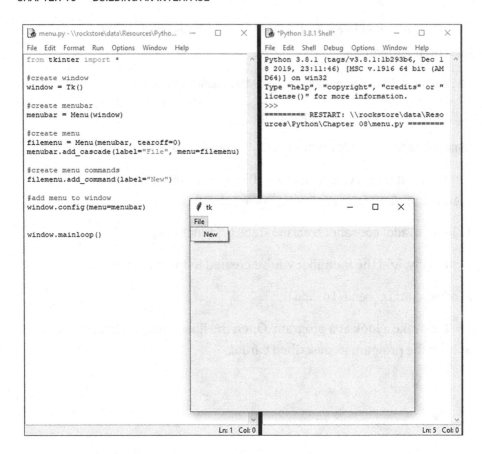

The Canvas

The canvas is used to draw and create graphics and layouts. This is where you place your graphics, text, buttons, and other widgets to create your interface.

To create a canvas, use

```
myCanvas = Tkinter.Canvas (parent-window, bg="sky blue",
height=300, width=300)
```

Use parent-window to attach the canvas to your window. Use height and width to size your canvas.

Use bg to set the background color. Open `colorchart.py` and run the program. This will create the color chart shown here.

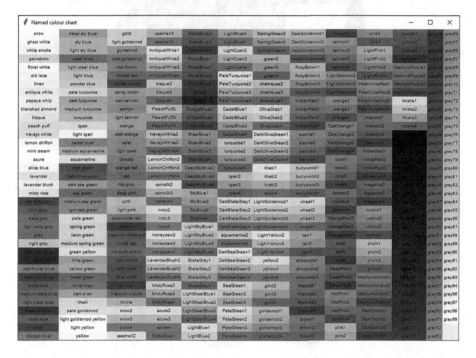

Select the name of the color from the chart to use in the bg parameter. Let's draw a shape on the canvas:

```
rect = myCanvas.create_rectangle
        (100, 100, 25, 50, fill="yellow")
```

The first two numbers are the x and y coordinates on the canvas. The second two numbers are the length and width.

You can also draw a polygon.

```
tri = myCanvas.create_polygon
        (100,150,  57,225,  143,225, fill="green")
```

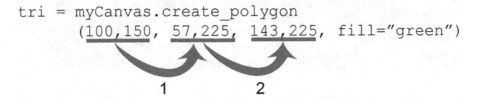

In this example, we're creating a triangle. A triangle has three sides, so we need to draw three lines. The first two numbers indicate the start point of the first line; the second two numbers indicate the end point of the first line, and so on. Let's take a look.

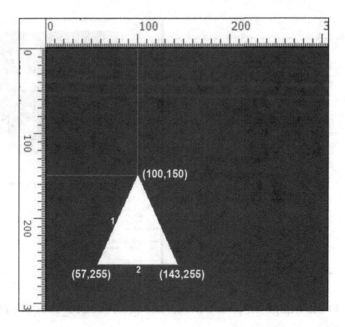

Try drawing a pentagon. A pentagon has five sides, so you need to draw five lines:

```
pent = myCanvas.create_polygon
    (100,150, 52,185, 71,240, 129,240, 148,185,
    fill="lime green")
```

Images

You can add images to your canvas. Have a look at images.py. To load the image, use the PhotoImage() function.

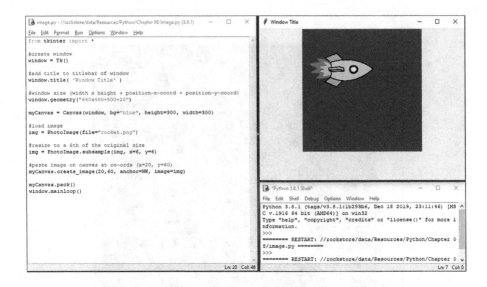

To paste the image on your canvas, use the `.create_image()` method.

Buttons

You can add command buttons to your canvas. To do this, use the Button() function.

Have a look at buttons.py:

```
myButton = Button(window, text="label", command)
```

Use window to specify the name of the window the button is to go on.

Use command to specify the function you want to call to handle what the button does. You can call existing functions or define your own functions to do this.

Use the `.pack` method to add the button to your window:

```
myButton.pack()
```

Message Boxes

You can add message boxes to your programs. To do this, you will need to import the message box functions from the Tkinter module. You can do this using the import command:

```
from tkinter import messagebox
```

You can create different types of message boxes: an info box, a warning box, an error box, and a box that asks for a yes/no response.

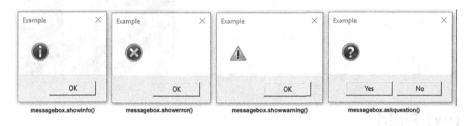

messagebox.showinfo()   messagebox.showerror()   messagebox.showwarning()   messagebox.askquestion()

```
messagebox.showinfo('Message Title', 'Message')
```

If you're asking the user for a yes/no response, you'll need to process this:

```
response = messagebox.askquestion
    ('Message Box' , 'Question...')
if response == 'yes' :
    executed if user clicks 'yes'
else :
    executed if user clicks 'no'
```

Let's have a look at messagebox.py.

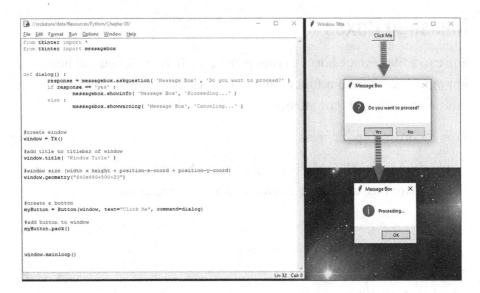

Text Field

Use the Entry() function to create your text field:

userInput = Entry(window)

Use the .pack() method to add the field to your window:

userInput.pack()

To get the data from the text field, use the .get() method:

userInput.get()

Let's add these to the program. Have a look at textfield.py. Here, we've added a text field to the canvas under the command button.

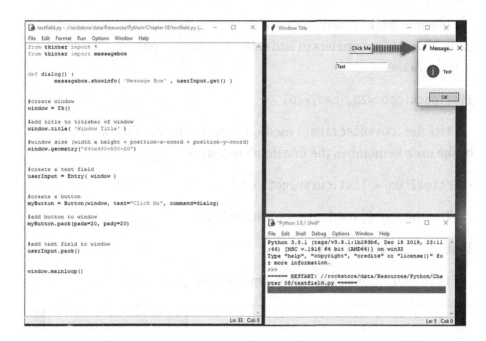

We've also added code in the `dialog()` function to get the data from the text field and display it in a message box.

The `dialog()` function is called when the "Click Me" button is clicked.

Run the program and see what it does.

Listbox

Use the `Listbox()` function to create your listbox:

```
list = Listbox(window)
```

Use the `.insert()` method to add items to the listbox:

```
list.insert(1, 'Item One')
```

Use the `.pack()` method to add the listbox to your window. Use the padx and pady parameters to add some padding to space out your listbox in the window.

```
list.pack(padx=20, pady=20)
```

Use the `.curselection()` method to get the index of the item selected by the user. Remember, the first item's index is 0.

```
selectedItem = list.curselection()
```

Use the `.get()` method to return the item:

```
list.get (selectedItem)
```

Let's take a look at a program. Open listbox.py.

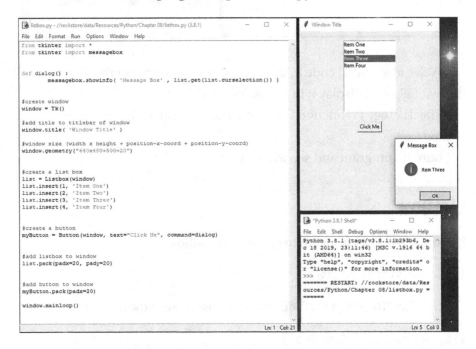

Checkbox

Use the Checkbutton()function to create each of your checkboxes:

```
box1 = Checkbutton(window, text="Red",
        variable=box1Checked, onvalue=1)
```

You'll need to create a variable for each checkbox to assign its "onvalue" if the user clicks the checkbox:

```
box1Checked = IntVar()
```

The variables you created will either be 1 or 0. Onvalue is set to 1, so the variable will be set to 1 when the user clicks the checkbox. Use the .get() method to get the value.

```
if box1Checked.get() == 1:
    messagebox.showinfo( 'Msg' , "Red" )
```

Use the .pack() method to add each of your checkboxes to your window:

```
box1.pack()
```

Let's take a look at a program. Open checkbox.py.

```
checkbox.py - //rockstore/data/Resources/Python/Chapter 08/checkbox.py (3.8.1)    —    □    ✕

File  Edit  Format  Run  Options  Window  Help
from tkinter import *
from tkinter import messagebox


def dialog() :
        if box1Checked.get() == 1:
                messagebox.showinfo( 'Message Box' , "Red" )
        if box2Checked.get() == 1:
                messagebox.showinfo( 'Message Box' , "Green" )
        if box3Checked.get() == 1:
                messagebox.showinfo( 'Message Box' , "Blue" )


#create window
window = Tk()

#add title to titlebar of window
window.title( 'Window Title' )

#window size (width x height + position-x-coord + position-y-coord)
window.geometry("640x480+500+20")


#create variable to assign 'onvalue' if checked
box1Checked = IntVar()
box2Checked = IntVar()
box3Checked = IntVar()

#create checkboxes
box1 = Checkbutton(window, text="Red", variable=box1Checked, onvalue=1)
box2 = Checkbutton(window, text="Green", variable=box2Checked, onvalue=1)
box3 = Checkbutton(window, text="Blue", variable=box3Checked, onvalue=1)

#add checkboxes to window
box1.pack()
box2.pack()
box3.pack()
```

When you run the program, you can select any of the checkboxes. When you click the button, the function reads which checkbox is selected and returns the value.

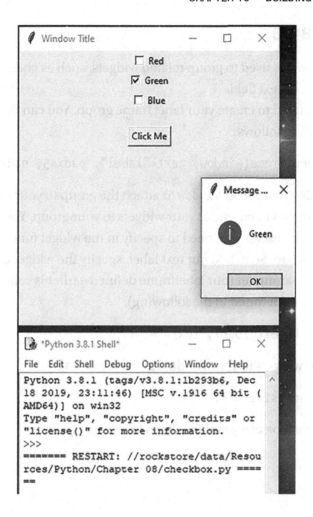

Labels

You can create labels to label text fields and other items on your interface. To do this, use Label():

```
textLabel = Label(window, text="Enter Name:")
```

Use pack() to add the label to your window:

```
textLabel.pack()
```

137

Label Frame

The LabelFrame is used to group related widgets, such as checkboxes, radio buttons, or text fields.

First, you need to create your label frame group. You can do this with LabelFrame() as follows:

```
group1 = LabelFrame(window, text="label", padx=5, pady=5)
```

Use the first parameter window to attach the group to your main window. Next, you need to add your widgets to your group. You can do this in the usual way, except you need to specify in the widget functions which widget to attach to. So to add our text label, specify the widget to attach to using the first parameter (our labelframe defined earlier is called group1, so use group1 underlined in the following).

```
textLabel = Label(group1, text="Name: ")
```

Add your widgets to your window in the usual way:

```
textLabel.pack(side=LEFT)
```

Let's take a look at a program. Open labelframe.py.

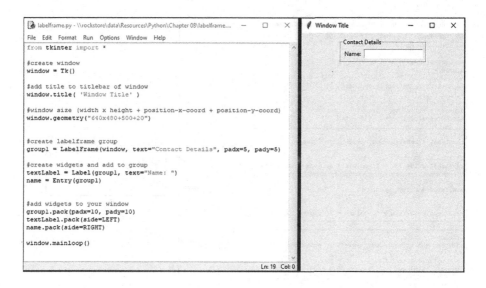

Here, we've created a text label and a text field inside the labelframe group (group1).

Interface Design

Now that we know how to create a window, menus, and add different types of widgets, we'll take a look at how to lay them out in the window to create a usable interface.

You can do this using the grid layout manager. Let's take a look at an example. Open the file gridlayout.py.

Use the `.grid()` method to place the widgets in the window according to the grid layout. Use `row` and `column` parameters to specify which cell in the grid to place the widget. Use the `padx` and `pady` parameters to add some spacing around your widgets in the grid.

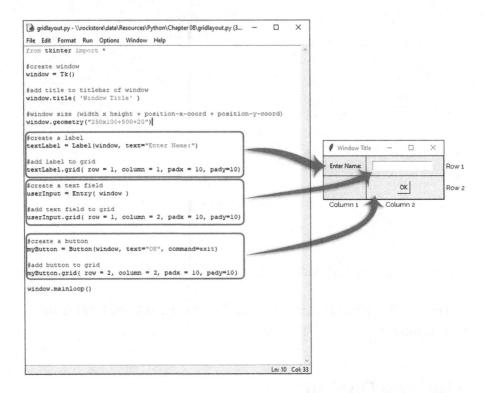

Here, we've placed a text label in row 1, column 1. There is a text field in row 1, column 2. We've placed a command button in row 2, column 2.

When you run the program, you'll see the result as shown here:

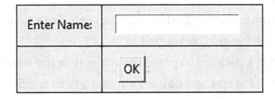

Let's design a simple interface for a unit converter app. To design this interface, we'll divide the window up into three rows and five columns.

◢	1	2	3	4	5
1			convert:	drop down	
2				text field	button
3				label	

Now, we'll place a logo on the left-hand side and span it across two columns and down three rows:

```
img = PhotoImage(file="logo.png")
imgLbl = Label(window, image=img)
imgLbl.grid( row = 1, column = 1, padx = 10,
   pady=10, columnspan=2, rowspan=3)
```

We'll also place a label in row 1, column 3:

```
textLabel = Label(window, text="Convert:")
textLabel.grid( row = 1, column = 3,
   padx = 10, pady=10)
```

A drop-down box in row 1, column 4:

```
conversions.grid( row = 1, column = 4, padx = 10, pady=10)
```

A text field in row 2, column 4, with a button in row 2, column 5:

```
userInput.grid( row = 2, column = 4, padx = 10, pady=10)
```

A label at the bottom in row 3, column 4, to show the result:

```
textLabel.grid( row = 3, column = 4, padx = 10, pady=5)
```

Add a command button to row 2, column 6:

```
myButton.grid( row = 2, column = 6,
   padx = 10, pady=10)
```

Let's take a look at the program. Open the file converter.py. Here, we're adding the widgets to the grid using the `.grid()` method.

```
converter.py - \\rockstore\data\Resources\Python\Chapter 08\converter.py (3.8.1)        —     □     ×

File  Edit  Format  Run  Options  Window  Help

#load image and add to imgLbl label
img = PhotoImage(file="logo.png")
imgLbl = Label(window, image=img)

#add image to grid
imgLbl.grid( row = 1, column = 1, padx = 10, pady=10, columnspan=2, rowspan=3)

#create a label
textLabel = Label(window, text="Convert:")

#add label to grid
textLabel.grid( row = 1, column = 3, padx = 10, pady=10)

#create drop down menu
conversions = Combobox(window, values=[
                              "Cm to Inch",
                              "Inch to Cm",
                              "Km to Miles",
                              "Miles to Km"])

#set combobox default selection
conversions.current(0)

#add combo box to grid
conversions.grid( row = 1, column = 4, padx = 10, pady=10)

#create a text field
userInput = Entry( window )

#add text field to grid
userInput.grid( row = 2, column = 4, padx = 10, pady=10)

#add label for result
textLabel = Label(window, text="")

#add result label to grid
textLabel.grid( row = 3, column = 4, padx = 10, pady=5)

#create a button
myButton = Button(window, text="OK", command=convert)

#add button to grid
myButton.grid( row = 2, column = 6, padx = 10, pady=10)

window.mainloop()

                                                            Ln: 14  Col: 29
```

We've used the padx and pady parameters to space out the widgets in the grid layout.

That's the interface sorted. As it stands, the program won't do anything if you click the button or enter a number into the text field.

We need to write a function to take care of this and call it when the button is clicked.

Declare the function in the usual way. We'll call this one convert().

```
def convert():
    if conversions.current() == 0:
        n = float(userInput.get()) * 0.39
        textLabel = Label(window, text=n)
        textLabel.grid( row = 3, column = 4, padx = 10, pady=5)
    elif conversions.current() == 1:
        n = float(userInput.get()) * 2.54
        textLabel = Label(window, text=n)
        textLabel.grid( row = 3, column = 4, padx = 10, pady=5)
    elif conversions.current() == 2:
        n = float(userInput.get()) * 0.62
        textLabel = Label(window, text=n)
        textLabel.grid( row = 3, column = 4, padx = 10, pady=5)
    elif conversions.current() == 3:
        n = float(userInput.get()) * 1.60
        textLabel = Label(window, text=n)
        textLabel.grid( row = 3, column = 4, padx = 10, pady=5)
```

You'll need to read the selection from the combo box. You can do this with the .current() method. The first item in the combo box has an index of 0, the second is 1, and so on. Use an if statement to separate the calculations for each selection in the combo box.

```
if conversions.current() == 0:
```

Next, you'll need to get the data from the text field. You can do this with a .get() method on the text field. Remember to cast the data type to a float, as the data from a text field is a string.

```
n = float (userInput.get())
```

Perform the calculation and return the result to the blank text label in row 3, column 4, of the grid.

Now, when you run the program, you'll get a nicely laid out interface.

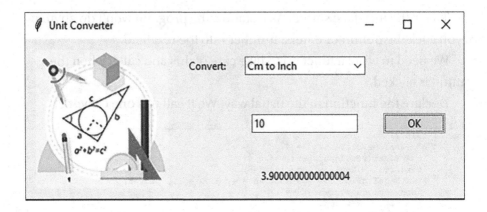

Summary

In this chapter, you learned the following:

- To create a graphical user interface using Python, you'll need to use Tkinter (Tk interface).

- Widgets are standard items for building a graphical user interface using Tkinter.

- The canvas is used to draw and create graphics and layouts. This is where you place your graphics, text, buttons, and other widgets to create your interface.

## CHAPTER 11

Developing a Game

To start creating your own games using Python, you'll need to use the pygame module. This module isn't bundled with standard distributions of Python, so you'll need to install it before you start.

Pygame is a library of Python modules designed for writing computer games. Pygame adds functionality to create fully featured games and multimedia applications using the Python language.

This chapter will cover the basic modules and functions that Pygame provides. We'll use these functions to create a very simple interactive game

Installing Pygame

To install the module, open a command prompt. Make sure you run this as an administrator. On the command prompt, type

```
pip install pygame
```

Once you press Enter, the install will begin.

© Kevin Wilson 2022
K. Wilson, *The Absolute Beginner's Guide to Python Programming*,
https://doi.org/10.1007/978-1-4842-8716-3_11

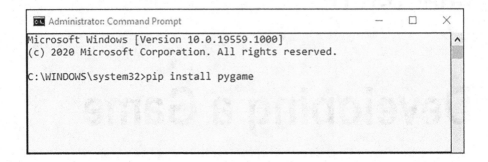

Allow the pip utility to download and install the module.

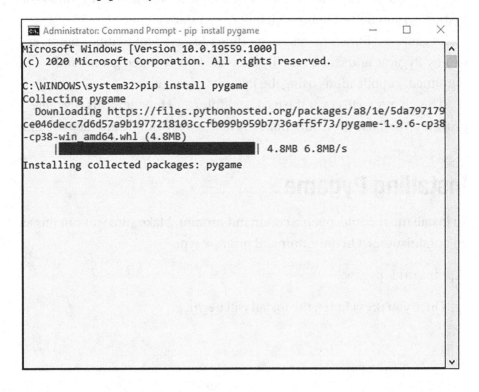

Once the process is complete, you can start using pygame.

Opening a Window

The first thing you'll need to do is import the pygame module:

```
import pygame
```

Initialize pygame using the .init() method:

```
pygame.init()
```

Open a window. This sets the window size 640 pixels wide by 480 pixels high. This could also be 800x600, 1920x1080, and so on.

```
gamewindow = pygame.display.set_mode((640,480))
```

Set the window's title. This is the title that appears in the title bar of the window.

```
pygame.display.set_caption("Game Window")
```

You should always end your pygame scripts with the .quit() method:

```
pygame.quit()
```

Let's take a look at the program so far.

```
*game01.py - \\rockstore\data\Resources\Python\C...    —    □    ×

File   Edit   Format   Run   Options   Window   Help

import pygame

pygame.init()

#create game window
gamewindow = pygame.display.set_mode((640,480))

#set window title
pygame.display.set_caption("Game Window")



pygame.quit()
```

If you run this program, the game window will initialize, open, and then immediately close. This is fine since there is no other code to execute.

Adding an Image

Let's add an image to the game window. This is going to be our character in the game. In this case, we're going to use a space rocket. We can add the image load statement to our program.

```
sprite = pygame.image.load('rocket.png')
```

Paste the image (sprite) onto the game window using the `.blit()` method, and assign the initial position on the screen (x, y):

```
gamewindow.blit(sprite, (x,y))
```

Update the display to show the image:

```
pygame.display.update()
```

Let's take a look at the program.

```
game04.py - \\rockstore\data\Resources\Python\Chapter 0...    —    □    ×

File   Edit   Format   Run   Options   Window   Help

import pygame

pygame.init()

gamewindow = pygame.display.set_mode((640,480))
pygame.display.set_caption("Game Window")

#load image and assign to 'sprite'
sprite = pygame.image.load('rocket.png')

#add image to game window
gamewindow.blit(sprite, (50,55))

#update the game window display
pygame.display.update()


pygame.quit()

                                                        Ln: 8   Col: 0
```

The Game Loop

Now, let's get our rocket ship to actually do something. To do this, we need to create a game loop to draw our sprites, update the screen, and keep the program running.

We can take the following two statements and add them to our game loop. For this bit, we'll use a while loop.

```
gamewindow.blit(sprite, (x,y))
```

Update the display to show the image:

```
pygame.display.update()
```

Put these inside the while loop:

```
while running == 1:
    gamewindow.blit(sprite, (x,y))
    pygame.display.update()
```

We'll also need to initialize some variables – x and y, the initial position on the screen, and running – to indicate whether the program is running or not:

```
running = 1
x = 250
y = 280
```

Let's take a look at the program.

```
#initialize our variables
running = 1
x=250
y=280

while running:
    #add image to game window
    gamewindow.blit(sprite, (x,y))

    #update the game window display
    pygame.display.update()


pygame.quit()
```

The Event Loop

In this simple game, we want the rocket ship to move left and right when the user presses the left and right arrow keys on the keyboard. To do this, we need something to handle these events.

To do this, we can put a for loop inside our while loop (the game loop). We're monitoring for each event that occurs. You can use the .get() method to read each event.

```
for event in pygame.event.get():
```

Now inside the for loop, we need some selection depending on which key is pressed. We can use an if statement for this.

First, we need to check whether a key has been pressed:

```
if event.type == pygame.KEYDOWN:
```

Inside this if statement, we need to identify which key has been pressed. You can use another if statement.

```
if event.key == pygame.K_LEFT:
```

We do the same for all other keys we're going to use. Just add elif statements to the if statement.

Let's take a look.

```
while running:

    for event in pygame.event.get():
        if event.type == pygame.KEYDOWN:
            if event.key == pygame.K_LEFT:
                x = x - 10 #shift image left 10 pixels
            elif event.key == pygame.K_RIGHT:
                x = x + 10 #shift image right 10 pixels

    gamewindow.blit(sprite, (x,y))
    pygame.display.update()


pygame.quit()
```

Ln: 18   Col: 0

Now, when we run the program, you'll see your rocket move left when you press the left key and right when you press the right key.

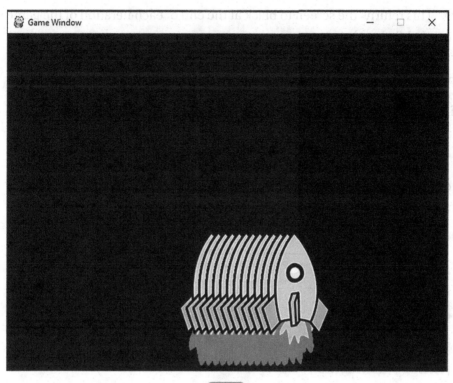

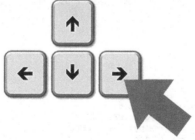

You'll also notice something else. The image repeats on the screen. To fix this, you need to clear the screen (refresh) each time you move the object. You can use

```
gamewindow.fill((0,0,0))
```

This returns the screen to black at the end of each iteration of the game loop (while loop).

It is also good practice to include a quit event in your event loop, so the program terminates gracefully:

```
if event.type == pygame.QUIT:
    running = 0
```

This will set our running variable to 0, meaning the game loop will terminate and the program will close. This event will happen when you click the close icon on the top right of the window.

Let's take a look at the program so far.

```
game10.py - //rockstore/data/Resources/Python/Chapter 09/game10.py (3.8.1)        —    □    ×
File  Edit  Format  Run  Options  Window  Help
import pygame

pygame.init()

gamewindow = pygame.display.set_mode((640,480))
pygame.display.set_caption("Game Window")

sprite = pygame.image.load('rocket.png')


#initialize our variables
running = 1
x=250
y=280


while running:

    for event in pygame.event.get():
        if event.type == pygame.KEYDOWN:
            if event.key == pygame.K_LEFT:
                x = x - 10 #shift image left 10 pixels
            elif event.key == pygame.K_RIGHT:
                x = x + 10 #shift image right 10 pixels
        if event.type == pygame.QUIT:
            running = 0 #close

    gamewindow.blit(sprite, (x,y))
    pygame.display.update()
    gamewindow.fill((0,0,0)) #clear screen

pygame.quit()
```

You'll also notice that the rocket doesn't move when you hold the key down. This is because the key-repeat feature is turned off. To turn this on, add the following line before your game loop:

```
pygame.key.set_repeat(1, 25)
```

The first parameter is the delay before the key event is repeated. The second parameter is the interval between repeats.

Shapes

You can add shapes such as circles, ellipses, rectangles, and other polygons.

To draw a rectangle, use the .rect() method. Specify the surface or window you want to draw on, the color, and then specify the x and y position, followed by the width and length of the rectangle.

```
pygame.draw.rect(gamewindow, colour,
    (x, y, width, length), thickness)
```

To draw an ellipse, use the .ellipse() method. When drawing an ellipse, you're actually drawing it inside an invisible rectangle. This is why you specify width and length when drawing your ellipse.

```
pygame.draw.ellipse(gamewindow, colour,
    (x, y, width, length), thickness)
```

To draw a circle, use the .circle() method. Specify the surface or window you want to draw on, the color, and then specify the x and y position, followed by the radius of the circle.

```
pygame.draw.circle(gamewindow, colour,
    (x, y), radius, thickness)
```

Have a look at shapes.py.

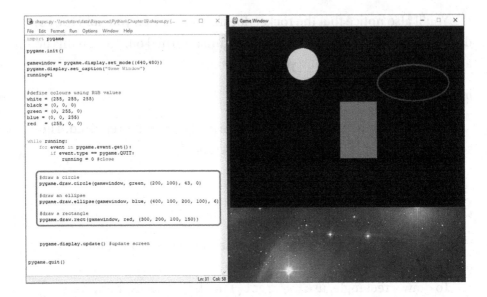

Basic Animation

To demonstrate basic animation, we're going to move our ufo object on the screen.

First, we need to load in our image. You can do this using the `.load()` method as we've done before.

```
ufo = pygame.image.load('ufo.png')
```

Now, because an image is loaded onto a surface object by default, we can't move it or manipulate it. To get around this, we assign the image to a rectangle. You can do this using the `.rect()` method.

```
ufo_rect = ufo.get_rect()
```

We also need to define some speed and direction variables. We can do this with a list. This is a list containing the [x, y] coordinates on the screen *(speed[0] is x, speed[1] is y)*.

```
speed = [10, 0]
```

To move the object, use the .move_ip() method:

```
ufo_rect.move_ip(speed)
```

Let's take a look at the program. Have a look at anim02.py.

```
#set horizontal by vertical list
speed = [10, 0]


#load ufo image
ufo = pygame.image.load('ufo.png')

#assign image to rectangle so we can manipulate its position
ufo_rect = ufo.get_rect()


#game loop
while running:

    #execute loop at 25 frames per second
    clock.tick(25)

    # move ufo
    ufo_rect.move_ip(speed)
```

Now, when you run this program, the ufo will fly from left to right across the screen.

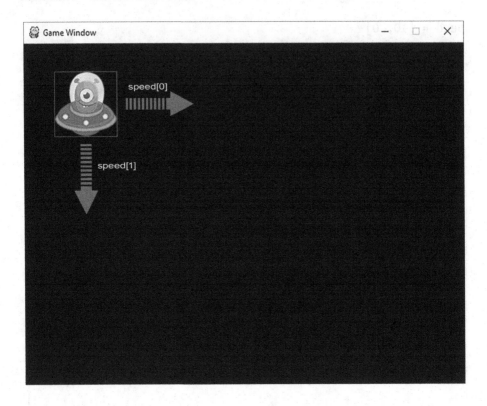

Because we set speed = [10, 0], this means we move our ufo ten pixels along the x axis each time we execute ufo_rect.move_ ip(speed) in the game loop.

If we set speed = [0, 10], this means we move our ufo ten pixels along the y axis each time we execute ufo_rect.move_ ip(speed) in the game loop.

Try changing the values in the program anim02.py and see what happens:

```
speed = [??, ??]
```

Try larger values.

Let's take our program a step further. Let's make the ufo bounce around the screen.

To do this, we need to check whether the left edge, right edge, top edge, and bottom edge of the ufo_rect go beyond the edges of the screen. We can use if statements for this.

If the left edge of the ufo goes off left edge, reverse x direction.

To reverse the direction, all you need to do is change the speed[0] to a negative number:

```
if ufo_rect.left < 0: speed[0] = -speed[0]
```

If the right edge of the ufo goes off right edge, reverse x direction.

Again, change the speed[0] to a negative number:

```
if ufo_rect.right > 640: speed[0] = -speed[0]
```

Do the same with the top and bottom. Give it a try.

159

Let's take a look at the program. Open anim03.py. Here, you'll see the ufo bounce around the screen.

```
#game loop
while running:

    #execute loop at 30 frames per second
    clock.tick(30)


    # move ufo by given offset (x,y)
    ufo_rect.move_ip(speed) #ufo_rect.move_ip (x, y)

    #bounce the ufo off the 4 edges
    #if ufo goes off left edge x reverse direction
    if ufo_rect.left < 0:
        speed[0] = -speed[0]

    #if ufo goes off right edge reverse x direction
    if ufo_rect.right > 640:
        speed[0] = -speed[0]

    #if ufo goes off top edge reverse y direction
    if ufo_rect.top < 0:
        speed[1] = -speed[1]

    #if ufo goes off bottom edge reverse y direction
    if ufo_rect.bottom > 480:
        speed[1] = -speed[1]
```

When the ufo moves toward the right wall, x (speed[0]) is increasing and y (speed[1]) is increasing.

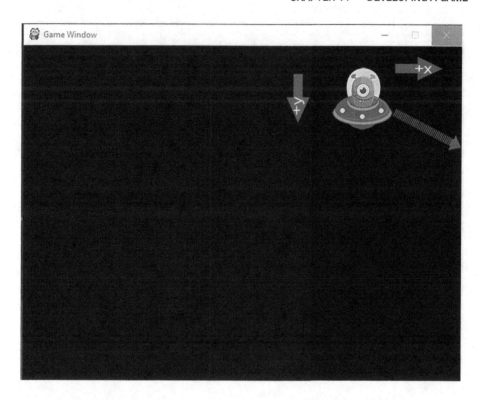

When the ufo hits the right wall, we change the direction of x
(speed[0]), but not y (speed[1]).

Now x (speed[0]) is decreasing, but y (speed[1]) is still increasing. Similarly for the other three sides.

What happens if you change the speed[ ] variables?

```
speed = [??, ??]
```

How would we add another ufo?

How would we add our rocket ship from the previous section?

To animate a character, you need to load your frames into a list:

```
frames = [pygame.image.load('frame1.png'),
          pygame.image.load('frame2.png'),
          pygame.image.load('frame3.png')]
```

Now, inside your main game loop, you can draw the frame using the .blit() method to draw the frame from the frames list:

```
gamewindow.blit(frames[counter], (x,y))
```

Select next frame in list, and loop back to first frame at the end of the list. We can do this with the len() function to return the number of frames in the list and modulus division.

```
counter = (counter + 1) % len(frames)
```

Let's take a look at the program. Open spriteanim.py.

```
spriteamin.py - \\rockstore\data\Resources\Python\Chapter 09\spriteamin.py (3.8.1)        —    □    ✕
File  Edit  Format  Run  Options  Window  Help
#turn on key repeat
pygame.key.set_repeat(1, 25)

counter=0
running=1
x=55
y=55

#load animation frames into list
frames = [pygame.image.load('frame1.png'),
          pygame.image.load('frame2.png'),
          pygame.image.load('frame3.png')]

#game loop
while running:
    #execute loop at 25 frames per second
    clock.tick(25)

    for event in pygame.event.get():
        if event.type == pygame.QUIT:
            running = 0 #close
        elif event.type == pygame.KEYDOWN:
            if event.key == pygame.K_LEFT:
                x = x - 10 #shift image right 10 pixels
            elif event.key == pygame.K_RIGHT:
                x = x + 10 #shift image right 10 pixels

    gamewindow.fill((0,0,0)) #clear screen

    gamewindow.blit(frames[counter], (x,y)) #redraw sprite in new position
    counter = (counter + 1) % len(frames) #move to next frame in frames list


    pygame.display.update() #update screen
```

With this particular animation, we have three frames to animate the flame effect on the rocket.

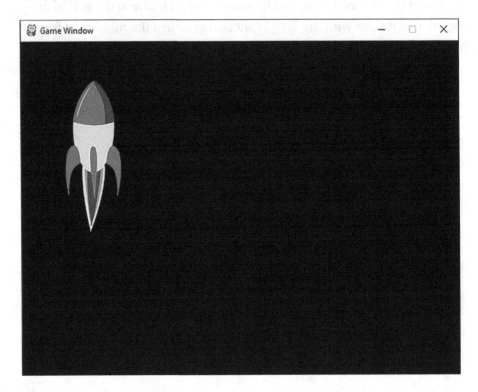

Summary

In this chapter, you learned that

- Pygame is a library of Python modules designed for writing computer games. Pygame adds functionality to create fully featured games and multimedia applications using the Python language.

- The game loop is used to draw our sprites, update the screen, and keep the program running.

- The event loop checks for events such as a keypress.

- The refresh rate is how fast the screen is redrawn.

## CHAPTER 12

Python Web Development

Python is widely used for developing large-scale web applications that are not possible to build using .NET and PHP.

Python supports features that are executed with different frameworks such as Django, Flask, Pyramid, and CherryPy commonly used in sites such Spotify and Mozilla.

You'll also need the source files in the directory Chapter11.

Web Servers

Most Python web applications are executed on a web server through an interface called WSGI (web server gateway interface). Other Python scripts are executed through CGI (common gateway interface).

Here, we've installed the Python interpreter and enabled the WSGI adapter module for the Apache web server.

© Kevin Wilson 2022
K. Wilson, *The Absolute Beginner's Guide to Python Programming*,
https://doi.org/10.1007/978-1-4842-8716-3_12

Client web browser   Server: 192.168.1.3

Figure 12-1. *An example of connecting to a web server on another machine*

For this section, you'll need access to a web server with Python support.

There is a free web server available from Aprelium called Abyss Web Server X1 that you can install on your computer to develop and test websites:

aprelium.com/downloads/

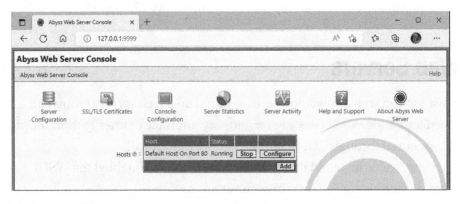

Figure 12-2. *The Aprelium web server running on a local computer*

Install the Web Server

1. Open the directory where you have saved the software package.

2. Double-click the software package icon.

3. Deselect components you do not want to install. Auto start enables Abyss Web Server auto starting when a Windows session starts – deselect this. Start Menu Shortcuts enables adding Abyss Web Server shortcuts in the Start Menu. Documentation installs help files.

4. Click Next.

5. Choose a directory where you want to install Abyss Web Server files. From now on, <Abyss Web Server directory> will refer to this directory.

6. Click Install.

Set Up Python Support

1. Open the Abyss Web Server's Console. Make sure the web server is running, then open your web browser, then enter the following in the address field at the top: 127.0.0.1:9999.

   Type in the admin password you created when you installed the server.

2. In the Hosts table, click Configure in the row corresponding to the host to which you want to add Python support.

3. Select Scripting Parameters.

4. Check Enable Scripts Execution.

5. Click Add in the Interpreters table.

6. Set Interface to CGI/ISAPI.

7. In the Interpreter field, click Browse..., go to the directory where you have installed Python, and click on python.exe.

8. Check Use the associated extensions to automatically update the Script Paths.

9. Click Add in the Associated Extensions table.

10. Enter py in the Extension field and click OK.

11. Click OK on interpreters screen.

12. Click OK in the Scripting Parameters screen.

13. Select Index Files.

14. Click Add in the Index Files table.

15. Enter index.pj in the File Name field, click OK. Then click OK in the index files screen.

16. Click Restart to restart the server.

Upload your scripts to your public_html directory on the server; then on your computer, open a web browser and enter the URL to your script:

```
http://server-name/script-name.py
```

For example:

```
http://titan/script.py
```

If you're using aprelium personal server on your own computer you can use

```
http://localhost/script.py
```

To start writing your Python scripts, you'll need to tell the web server where to find the Python interpreter. This is usually

```
#!/python/python
```

or on a Linux server

```
#!/usr/bin/python
```

This is the first line of your script.

Executing a Script

Let's take a look at an example. Have a look at script.py. Here, we've written a script to output a simple HTML page.

```
script.py - \\titan\www\script.py (3.8.1)    —    □    ×
File  Edit  Format  Run  Options  Window  Help
#!/python/python

print ('Content-type:text/html\r\n\r\n')
print ('<!doctype html>')
print ('<html>')
print ('<head>')
print ('<meta charset="utf-8">')
print ('<title>Python</title>')
print ('</head>')
print ('<body>')
print ('<h1>It works!!')
print ('</body>')
print ('</html>')
```

This page simply outputs the heading "It works!!." Upload the script into your public_html directory on your web server, and then navigate to the script URL using your web browser on your computer.

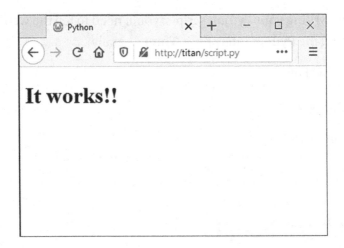

In our lab URL, this would be

`http://titan/script.py`

Let's take a look at a practical example. Here, we're creating a simple contact form. The user is presented with an HTML form that asks for their name, email address, and a message.

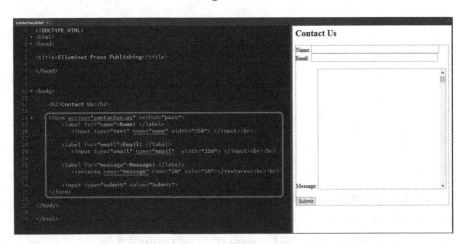

When the user clicks the "Submit" button, the HTML form calls a Python script called contactus.py.

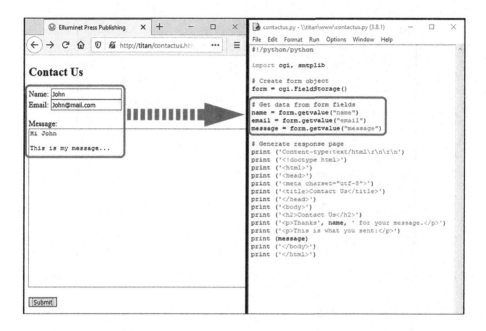

The Python script processes the data passed from the HTML form and stores it in a form object.

We can then get the values passed from the HTML form and store them in this object.

The Python script generates another HTML page using print statements for the response to the user.

```
contactus.py - \\titan\www\contactus.py (3.8.1)        —      □      ×

File   Edit   Format   Run   Options   Window   Help
#!/python/python

import cgi, smtplib

# Create form object
form = cgi.FieldStorage()

# Get data from form fields
name = form.getvalue("name")
email = form.getvalue("email")
message = form.getvalue("message")

# Generate response page
print ('Content-type:text/html\r\n\r\n')
print ('<!doctype html>')
print ('<html>')
print ('<head>')
print ('<meta charset="utf-8">')
print ('<title>Contact Us</title>')
print ('</head>')
print ('<body>')
print ('<h2>Contact Us</h2>')
print ('<p>Thanks', name, ' for your message.</p>')
print ('<p>This is what you sent:</p>')
print (message)
print ('</body>')
print ('</html>')
```

You can see the output in the following browser.

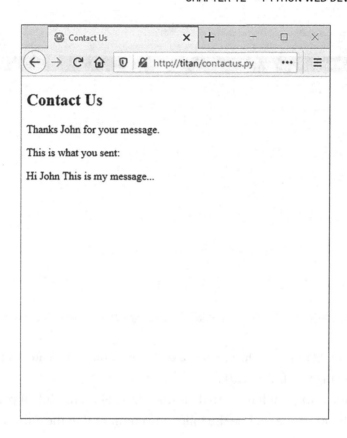

Python Web Frameworks

If you are using Python in web development, you'll more than likely be using a Python web framework rather than the old CGI we looked at in the previous section.

A Python web framework is a collection of tools, libraries, and technologies that allow you to build a web application.

One example of a Python web framework is Django (pronounced "Jango").

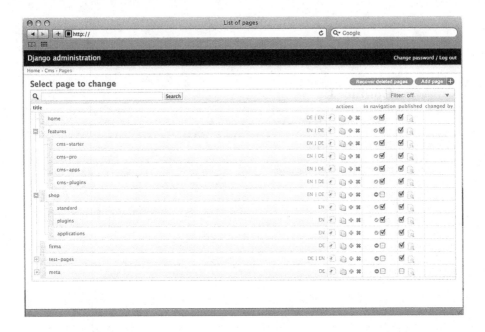

Another example is Flask. Let's take a look at how to create a simple web app using this framework.

The first thing you'll need to do is install the Flask module if you haven't already done so. Use the following command in the admin command prompt:

```
pip install Flask
```

Use this if you're on a Linux-based machine:

```
sudo pip install Flask
```

Let's create an app. First thing we need to do is create our main program. To do this, we create a new file called app.py. We've included all these files in the Flask directory in the resource files.

```
app.py - \\rockstore\data\Resources\Python\Chapter 11\fl...    —    □    ×

File   Edit   Format   Run   Options   Window   Help

from flask import Flask

app = Flask(__name__)

@app.route('/')
def index():
    return 'This is a Flask Web App'

if __name__ == '__main__':
    app.run(debug=True, host='0.0.0.0')
|

                                                        Ln: 11   Col: 0
```

Here, we've imported our Flask module.

Modern web apps use a technique called routing. This means instead of having a URL to a page

```
localhost/resources.php
```

we use a route

```
localhost/resources/
```

So our first route is the root of our website and is usually the index page. We use @app.route('/') to determine this.

The "/" means the root of the website:

```
http://localhost:5000/
```

def index() is the name you give to the route defined earlier. This one is called index, because it's the index (or home page) of the website.

177

host='0.0.0.0' means the app is accessible from any machine on the network.

To run and test the app, we need to open it using the development environment. This is a simple web server that allows you to open the app in a web browser for testing.

To do this, open your app directory in the command prompt. In this particular example, the app files are in OneDrive/Documents/Flask.

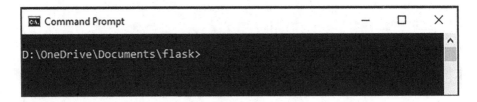

To start the app, type

```
python app.py
```

Once you press Enter, the server will start.

```
D:\OneDrive\Documents\flask>python app.py
 * Serving Flask app "app" (lazy loading)
 * Environment: production
   WARNING: This is a development server. Do not use it in a production deployment.
   Use a production WSGI server instead.
 * Debug mode: on
 * Restarting with stat
 * Debugger is active!
 * Debugger PIN: 129-355-584
 * Running on http://0.0.0.0:5000/ (Press CTRL+C to quit)
```

You can open the app in a web browser. On your own workstation, you can use localhost:5000:

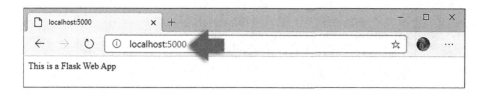

To add another page, add another route.

```
@app.route('/shop')
def shop():
        return 'This is the shop page'
```

Now in the web browser, you can use

localhost:5000/shop

Now that we have our base app, we can develop web pages for the
app to call. These web pages are called templates and we store these in a
template directory. Here's a simple HTML page we've created and saved in
the templates directory.

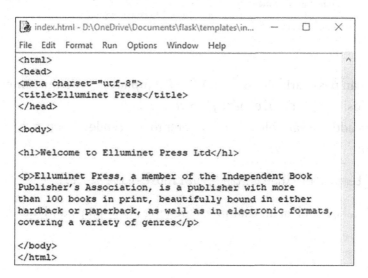

Let's call our HTML page from our app. We can use the render_
template() function.

```
app02.py - D:\OneDrive\Documents\flask\app02.py (3.8.1)    —    ☐    ✕

File  Edit  Format  Run  Options  Window  Help

from flask import Flask, render_template

app = Flask(__name__)

@app.route('/')
def index():
    return render_template('index.html')


if __name__ == '__main__':
    app.run(debug=True, host='0.0.0.0')
```

When we view the page in a browser, we'll see a rendered version of the HTML page.

Welcome to Elluminet Press Ltd

Elluminet Press, a member of the Independent Book Publisher's Association, is a publisher with more than 100 books in print, beautifully bound in either hardback or paperback, as well as in electronic formats, covering a variety of genres

You can pass variables to your HTML templates. To do this, embed the variable using {{variable-name}} in your HTML.

Then add the variable as a parameter to the render_template() function:

```
render_template('index.html', variable-name = "...")
```

Let's take a look at an example. Open the file app3.py and index2.html.

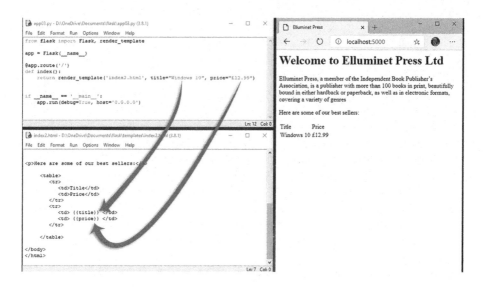

Here, we've passed the title and price as variables to the HTML template.

You can add images to your templates using HTML and CSS code. You can also embed Python code.

Summary

In this chapter, you learned that

- Django, Flask, Pyramid, and CherryPy are common Python web development frameworks.

- Most Python web applications are executed on a web server through an interface called WSGI (web server gateway interface).

APPENDIX A

Quick Reference

Some of the most commonly used data types, operators, methods, functions, and loop constructs to help you when writing your programs.

Data Types

```
int = 45
float = 45.2123
str = "this is a string"
list = [ item1, item2, ... ]
tuple = ( item1, item2, ... )
dict = { key1:item1, key2:item2, ...}
bool = True / False
```

Numeric Operators

Division	/
Modulus Division	%
Multiplication	*
Exponent	**
Addition	+
Subtraction	-

© Kevin Wilson 2022
K. Wilson, *The Absolute Beginner's Guide to Python Programming*,
https://doi.org/10.1007/978-1-4842-8716-3

Comparison Operators

Equal to	==
Not equal to	!=
Greater than	>
Greater than or equal to	>=
Less than	<
Less than or equal to	<=

Boolean Operators

not
and
or

String Operators

retrieve char at index	string[index]
retrieve char in range	string[a:b]

List Operators

define list	list = []
assign x to list	list[index] = x
retrieve from list	list[index]
retrieve last item	list[-1]
return items in range	list[a:b]

Dictionary Operators

```
define dictionary          dict = {}
assign x to key in dict    dict[key] = x
retrieve item at key       dict[key]
```

String Methods

```
convert to uppercase    .upper()
convert to lowercase    .lower()
return length of x      .len(x)
Count times x occurs    .count(x)
```

List Methods

```
add x to end of list    .append(x)
insert x at y           .insert(y,x)
pop item at x off list  .pop(x)
clear all items         .clear()
remove x from list      .remove(x)
```

Dictionary Methods

```
return value at key   .get(key)
remove item           .pop(item)
display all values    .values()
```

Functions

```
def function(<parameters>):
    <function code>
    return <data>
```

Files

```
open file              open(<file>,<mode>)
read file              .read()
read 1 line at a time  .readline()
close file             .close()
write data to file     .write(<data>)
loop through lines     for line in file:
<code>
```

Conditional

```
if <condition> :
    <code>
else:
    <code>
```

Multi-conditional

```
if <condition> :
    <code>
elif <condition> :
    <code>
```

While Loop

```
while <condition>:
    <code>
```

For Loop

```
for <variable> in range:
    <code>
```

Loop Control

break current loop   break
continue to next iteration   continue

Modules

```
import module
from module import *
```

Built-In Functions

get input from console   input()
print data to console   print(x)
convert x to integer   int(x)
convert x to float   float(x)
convert x to string   str(x)
convert x to list   list(x)
range a-b increments of c   range(a,b,c)

Declare a Class

```
class class-name:
    def____init____(self, <parameters>):
        <initialize attributes>
            <methods>
```

Child Class

```
class child-class(parent-class):
```

Create Object

```
object = class-name(<parameters>)
```

Call Object Method

```
object.method-name(<parameters>)
```

Access Object Attributes

```
object-name.attribute-name
```

Exceptions

```
try:
    # Code to execute as normal except
exception (exception name]:
    # Code to deal with exception
```

Index

A

Animation
    .blit() method, 162
    direction, 159, 161
    edges, 159
    frames, 162
    len() function, 163
    .load() method, 156
    .move_ip() method, 157
    program, 160, 163
    .rect () method, 156
    speed, 156, 158, 162
    values, 158
Arithmetic operators, 42
    performing, 43
    precedence, 42

B

BIDMAS, 42
Binary file, 79
    file modes, 72
    open() method, 79, 80
    pickle.dump() method, 81
    pickle.read() method, 81, 82
    .write() method, 80, 81

Bitwise operators, 45
BODMAS, 42
Boolean operators, 44
break statement, 68

C

Classes, 109–111
Class inheritance
    child class, 114
    definition, 113
    dot notation, 116
    lecturer object, 115
    Person class, 113, 114
    super() class, 114
Common gateway interface (CGI),
    167, 175
Comparison operators, 43–44
Computer programming
    install on Linux, 11–13
    install on MacOS, 9–11
    install on windows, 4, 6–9
    languages, 1
    Python, 2, 3
    variables/constants, 1
continue statement, 68

© Kevin Wilson 2022
K. Wilson, *The Absolute Beginner's Guide to Python Programming*,
https://doi.org/10.1007/978-1-4842-8716-3

D

Data type, 32
   casting, 41
   dictionary, 38, 39
   floating point number, 33
   integer, 32
   lists, 33, 34
   sets, 37
   strings, 33
   tuples, 37, 38

E

elif statement, 55, 57, 60
else statements, 52–54
Exceptions
   catching, 105–107
   definition, 103
   raising, 107, 108
   types, 103–105
   uses, 103

F

File access
   .seek() method, 83
   text file, 83
   values, 83
Flow control, 49
for loop, 61–65, 151
Functions
   declaration, 87–89
   definition, 87
   recursive, 90–92

G

Global variables, 32, 90
Graphical user interface
   designing
      command button, 141
      convert() function, 143
      .current() method, 143
      .get() method, 143
      .grid() method, 142
      label, 141
      logo, 141
      Program, run, 143
      text field, 141
      window, 140
   .geometry() method,
      121, 123
   .grid() method, 139
   parameters, 139
   result, 140
   Tk() function, 122
   Tkinter, 121
   widgets (*see* Widgets)
   window
      creation, 121
      .mainloop()
         method, 123
      position, 122
      size, 122
      .title() method, 123

H

High-level language,
   2, 16–18

I, J, K

if statements, 52–55
Input data, 40
Integrated development
    environment (IDE), 3
Integrated development
    environment (IDLE), 8, 9,
    12, 15, 22
Iteration
    for loop, 61–64
    while loop, 65, 66

L

Language classification
    high-level, 16–18
    low-level, 15, 16
Lists, 33–34
Local variables, 31, 32
Logical operators, 44
Low-level language, 15–16

M, N

Method overriding, 110, 117–119
Modules, 96
    creation, 100, 101
    definition, 96
    importing, 97
        dot notation, 97, 98
        forward() function, 97, 98
        import keyword, 96
        namespace, 97

output, 98
right () function, 97
turtle commands, 100

O

Object-oriented
    programming (OOP)
    abstraction, 110
    encapsulation, 109
    inheritance, 110
    polymorphism, 110
Objects, 80, 109–113
Output data, 34, 36, 40, 41

P, Q

Polymorphic classes, 116–117
Polymorphism, 109, 110
Pygame
    event loop
        elif statements, 151
        .get() method, 151
        if statement, 151
        parameters, 155
        program, 152, 154
        termination, 154
    game loop, 149, 150
    image, adding, 148
    installation, 145, 146
    window, opening, 147, 148
Python, 2, 3, 18, 96, 109,
    167, 175

Python language syntax
    code fragment, 29
    comments, 20, 21
    escape character, 21, 22
    identifiers, 20, 29
    indentation, 20
    input, 21
    output, 21
    reserved words, 18, 19
    write a program, 22–28
Python supports, 167–171

R

Recursive function, 90–92

S

Scope
    global, 90
    local, 90
script.py
    contact form, 172
    contactus.py, 172
    HTML, 171, 173
    output, 174
    uploading, 171
    URL, 172
Selection
    elif statements, 55, 57, 60
    if/else statements, 52–54
Sequence, 49–52
Sets, 37

Second-generation programming
    language, 15
Shapes, 155–156
Streaming services, 2
Strings, 33

T, U

Text file
    characters, 73
    .close( ) method, 77
    file modes, 72
    open( ) method, 73, 74
    .read() method, 78, 79
    .write ( ) method, 75–77
Two-dimensional lists, 35, 36

V

Variables, 1, 31
    global, 32
    local, 31

W, X, Y, Z

Web frameworks
    app3.py/index2.html, 180, 181
    definition, 175
    Django, 175
    Flask, 176
    render_ template()
        function, 179
    templates, 179

variable, adding, 180
web app
    app.py, 176
    def index(), 177
    Flask module, 176
    localhost, 178
    routing, 177
    run/test, 178
Web server gateway interface
    (WSGI), 167
Web servers
    Abyss Web Server X1, 168
    connections, 168

installation, 169
while loop, 49, 65–69, 149–151
Widgets
    buttons, 130
    canvas, 126–129
    checkboxes, 135, 136
    images, 129, 130
    LabelFrame, 138, 139
    labels, 137
    listbox, 133, 134
    menus, 124, 125
    message boxes, 131
    text field, 132, 133

Printed in the United States
by Baker & Taylor Publisher Services

Printed in the United States
by Baker & Taylor Publisher Services